D0205135

"Here is a portable apologetic toolkit that ough... standard equipment in the backpack of every Christian university student. In crisp, readable prose, I am eager to offer this volume as a handy, accessible resource to students drowning in a sea of secularism."

—ROBERT OSBURN
Ph.D. candidate, University of Minnesota, and executive director of The MacLaurin Institute

"If you want to be conversation-ready with convenient summaries drawn from fine Christian minds, study this book. By absorbing these synopses, you will be ready to answer anyone who asks, seeks or knocks for reasons."

—RAMESH RICHARD PH.D., TH.D.
professor, Dallas Theological Seminary and president, RREACH International

5 MINUTE Apologist

MAXIMUM TRUTH
IN MINIMUM TIME

DR. RICK CORNISH

NAVPRESS®

BRINGING TRUTH TO LIFE

OUR GUARANTEE TO YOU

The Navigators is an international Christian organization. Our mission is to reach, disciple, and equip people to know Christ and to make Him known through successive generations. We envision multitudes of diverse people in the United States and every other nation who have a passionate love for Christ, live a lifestyle of sharing Christ's love, and multiply spiritual laborers among those without Christ.

NavPress is the publishing ministry of The Navigators. NavPress publications help believers learn biblical truth and apply what they learn to their lives and ministries. Our mission is to stimulate spiritual formation among our readers.

ISBN 1-57683-505-7

Cover design by Arvid Wallen
Creative Team: Don Simpson, Rachelle Gardner, Arvid Wallen, Darla Hightower, Glynese Northam

Some of the anecdotal illustrations in this book are true to life and are included with the permission of the persons involved. All other illustrations are composites of real situations, and any resemblance to people living or dead is coincidental.

Unless otherwise identified, all Scripture quotations in this publication are taken from the HOLY BIBLE: NEW INTERNATIONAL VERSION® (NIV®), copyright © 1973, 1978, 1984 by International Bible Society, used by permission of Zondervan Publishing House, all rights reserved. Other versions include: the *New King James Version* (NKJV), copyright © 1982 by Thomas Nelson, Inc., used by permission, all rights reserved and the *New Revised Standard Version* (NRSV), copyright 1989, by the Division of Christian Education of the National Council of the Churches of Christ in the USA, used by permission, all rights reserved.

Cornish, Rick, 1950-
  5 minute apologist : maximum truth in minimum time / Rick Cornish.-- 1st ed.
     p. cm.
  Includes bibliographical references and index.
  ISBN 1-57683-505-7
  1. Apologetics. I. Title: Five minute apologist. II. Title.
  BT1103.C67 2005
  239--dc22
                                    2004024619

Printed in Canada
1 2 3 4 5 6 7 8 9 10 / 10 09 08 07 06 05

To my wife, Tracy, who fought and won against cancer during the year I wrote this book. Her steady faith during that time symbolizes her lifelong commitment to the truth of Christianity.

Always be prepared to give an answer to everyone who asks you to give the reason for the hope that you have. (1 PETER 3:15)

Contents

Foreword

Rational argument used to be an ally of the Christian faith. In particular, it was thought that sound reasoning and powerful evidence supported the key claims of Christianity. If people rejected these teachings, it was assumed they weren't thinking clearly, and not, as we now suppose, that their heads were telling them one thing and their hearts another. It's worth remembering that until two centuries ago, most people in the West saw the Resurrection of Jesus in historically the same light as other events of antiquity, such as the murder of Julius Caesar. The Resurrection and Caesar's murder were both regarded as equally factual and historical.

Unfortunately, in the two hundred years since the Enlightenment, Christians have steadily retreated from seeing their faith as rationally compelling. Instead of being apologists for the faith, we have become apologetic about it. We tend to think that the reasons for rejecting Christianity are at least as strong as those for accepting it. After all, so many "smart people" now reject the faith. Moreover, these "skeptics" have developed a veritable arsenal for dismantling the Christian faith, everything from biblical criticism, which purports to show that the

Bible cannot be trusted, to advances in modern science, which some use to claim that God's role in nature is dispensable.

As a consequence, many Christians now take a dim view of apologetics, dismissing it as merely "arguing people into faith." But this misses the point. Arguments, in the sense of sustained reasoned reflection, can be vehicles for either helping bring about faith or destroying it. Many young people, as they go off to school, lose their faith because they are presented with arguments declaring that Christianity is false. Sound arguments that show the reasonableness of Christianity can be of immense help to struggling students trying to determine whether their faith is true. Yes, our salvation is ultimately due to the grace of God. But every act of divine grace presupposes the *means of grace* by which God makes His grace real to us. Christian apologetics is one such means of grace.

As a means of divine grace, apologetics cannot be blithely dismissed as something Christians can safely ignore. Indeed, throughout Scripture, Christians are enjoined to defend the faith through rational argument. Thus, Peter urged, "Always be ready to make your defense [*apologia*] to anyone who demands from you an accounting for the hope that is in you" (1 Peter

3:15, NRSV). Likewise, Paul understood his own ministry as constituting a "defense [*apologia*] and confirmation [*bebaiosis*] of the Gospel" (Philippians 1:7, NRSV). The Greek *apologia* denotes a legal defense, and the Greek *bebaiosis* means verification or proof.

The Roman statesman Seneca observed, "If you want a man to keep his head when crisis comes, you must give him some training before it comes." Our secular culture breeds many a crisis of faith. It is common for young people who are enthusiastic about serving God to leave home, get exposed to faulty teaching, and turn away from the truth of Christianity. People need to be equipped to handle the assaults on heart and mind that they encounter at school, in the workplace, on television, and just about everywhere they look. Rick Cornish's *5 Minute Apologist* is a useful primer in Christian apologetics for those who are finding their faith assaulted. Whether you are beleaguered with doubts about the truth of Christianity, or simply want to learn how to defend your faith, this is a great place to begin your training in apologetics.

WILLIAM A. DEMBSKI
Baylor University
Author of *The Design Revolution*

Introduction

Some years ago, in a conversation with another Christian, I mentioned the evidence for Jesus' resurrection. Based on objective, historical facts, I said I was convinced that Jesus really died and came back to life. His response surprised me: "Well, I never actually thought of it that way." He preferred to think of the Resurrection as a "matter of faith." Consideration of the evidence seemed to shake his "faith" rather than support it.

Some Christians may not be sure of the objective truth of Christianity, or may even be threatened by it. Some think of it simply as their religion, without reflecting on whether or not it's true in an absolute sense. If that's the case for some Christians, imagine how non-Christians view it.

Christianity no longer enjoys the cultural acceptability it once did. In America's past, little challenge was raised. We could reasonably assume that most people had been exposed to Christianity, and even if they rejected it, they understood what it was. Not so today. Many Americans live in willful rejection and defiance of America's Christian heritage. We are thus swamped with alternate religions, dangerous cults, and competing philosophies.

What makes the marketplace of ideas more challenging than ever is that today the very concept of truth is often rejected. The assumed position among the "enlightened" is pluralism—not just the awareness of multiple options, but the assumption that all views are equally true. We make our own truth. We believe whatever we want, and our argument for it is valid because we simply want it to be. Thus we are "tolerant" of every perspective, except views that are exclusive, that is, those who believe they possess the one and only Truth. Usually, that's code for the historic Christian faith.

The need for apologetics has never been greater. And the biblical mandate still rings clear: "Always be prepared to give an answer to everyone who asks you to give the reason for the hope that you have" (1 Peter 3:15). The word translated "answer" comes from the Greek word *apologia*, the origin of "apologetics" in English. Peter is commanding us *not* to make an apology, but to prepare to give a defense for the Christian faith.

Considering the competitive nature of the marketplace of ideas, it seems that few churches adequately prepare their people to defend the faith. It's much easier and more pleasant to stay within the church walls, pat one another on the back, and just make ourselves feel good. As long as we ensure that our young people stay within those walls, we can ignore the battle that rages outside. But young people grow up, go to college, and enter that marketplace of ideas. Even if they try to flee the intellectual war raging around us, it will find them. Have we prepared them?

Research indicates that up to 80 percent of evangelical kids lose their faith in college. What happened in our churches and youth groups to allow that? No nation would willingly take 80 percent casualties in a war. Why do we? If we don't train our people, especially our young people, in apologetics, we'll lose this war, at least in America. Some believe we already have.

Ironically, we live in a time of great Christian apologists, defenders of our faith. They have produced terrific resources to prepare us for spiritual and intellectual combat. But as with theology, many Christians in the pew don't read and study the great works available to us. Lack of time seems to be the most common excuse for not preparing in more depth. That's why I've written *5 Minute Apologist* in small chunks to fit into short time frames. The first book in this series (*5 Minute Theologian*) explains *what* Christians have historically believed. This book gives reasons *why* we believe it. I hope it serves as a springboard to more serious apologetics study.

The *5 Minute* series originally germinated out of

my concern that my sons, Scott and Ben, would be as prepared as possible to face the world as thinking Christians. Part of that preparation was at least a basic awareness of apologetics issues. Other parents who read some of what I put together for my boys asked for copies for their kids, and then urged me to write more.

I also felt compelled to write these books because of the experience I had when I taught in a Christian college in the former Soviet Union. In that very different culture, I observed the deeper thinking and more inquisitive minds of students in the post-Soviet world. Even without religious freedoms in their earlier years, they were still better prepared to argue for their faith than many students in the West who neglect their opportunities to do the same. Our high school graduates are simply unprepared to enter university life as Christians.

My final reason for writing the *5 Minute* series was that as a former pastor, I was shocked to find Christians who don't even know the word "apologetics," let alone know how to use it (or in some cases even care). Why would we be surprised that our culture has gone in the tank, Christianly speaking, when people who claim to follow Christ are not only ignorant of the evidence to support Christianity, but apathetic as well?

Even though I initially aimed at high school students, I believe that *5 Minute Apologist* fills a need for inquisitive Christians of all ages. Each chapter is short enough to be read in five minutes, like a devotional. By reading (and re-reading) one each day, the Christian can boost his or her apologetics awareness considerably in about three months. I have tried to include as much core information and as little fluff in each chapter as possible. Thus the subtitle, *Maximum Truth in Minimum Time.*

I also hope this will be a helpful resource for parents to use with their kids before other worldviews and "isms" grab their minds and hearts. It is also suited for youth groups, Christian schools, and homeschoolers who want an introduction to apologetics issues. As with *5 Minute Theologian*, the format is a small, easily useable resource to take to college for quick reference.

The chapters are not intended to be full arguments of the issues. Space does not allow that. But they provide background context—a foundational framework—from which the Christian can launch into further research. Part 1 sets the stage by dealing with thinking. If we don't think well, we can't explore any topic with confidence in our findings. Part 2 considers support for the Bible, the written source of Christian truth. If it can't stand, all the rest falls. Part 3 introduces worldviews, alternate sets of assumptions that guide how people view reality. Understanding others' interpretive lens helps us play the game better on their home field. God is the topic of part 4. Everything ultimately centers around the question of whether or not He is there.

Christian apologetics does not try to defend generic religion, but Jesus. So part 5 discusses topics about Him, ground zero of the Christian faith. Part 6 concentrates on His resurrection. If it didn't happen, Christianity is bogus. Part 7 introduces some issues raised by one of Christianity's main challengers today—science. Miracles are the topic of part 8. Can we really believe they happened? Part 9 introduces many of the world's other religions, which are no longer isolated to their countries of origin, but are found around the globe. Bizarre and sometimes dangerous new religious movements are found in part 10.

5 Minute Apologist will not arm the Christian with everything needed to wade into the spiritual warfare of our pluralistic world. The challenges are too many and diverse for one book to do that. But I hope it provides an introduction to the issues that threaten our faith. If it provides a platform for further study and preparation, it will have served its purpose.

Ideas Have Consequences

Peter commands Christians to know and use apologetics: "Always be prepared to give an answer to everyone who asks you to give the reason for the hope that you have" (1 Peter 3:15). Obedience to this Spirit-inspired directive requires thinking. One of God's greatest gifts to mankind is the human mind—our capacity to think and communicate ideas. Thinking drives life. Our ideas result in consequences in our lives and others' lives. The apostle Paul realized that ideas could revolutionize our lives: "Be transformed by the renewing of your mind" (Romans 12:2).

The Bible connects thoughts and actions. Consequences result from actions, but they germinate in our thoughts. Choices and actions don't just spring into the external world from a vacuum. They originate from ideas in the mind. Jesus said our evil deeds come from inside: "For out of the heart come evil thoughts, murder, adultery, sexual immorality, theft, false testimony, slander" (Matthew 15:19).

Ideas bear observable consequences in the real

world. A person who believes that gravity doesn't apply to him may jump off a building. Someone who believes moving vehicles can't hurt him may step in front of one. Some people who follow deranged cult leaders like Jim Jones commit suicide. On the positive side, ideas in the field of biochemistry lead to cures for diseases. Ideas about making and selling products lead to jobs. Ideas about God lead to worship.

Ideas shape history. Charles Darwin's theory of evolution affected not only the biological sciences, but the social sciences. Friedrich Nietzsche's nihilistic philosophy formed part of the seedbed of the Nazi regime. Comparing the two sides of Berlin before the Wall fell reveals the consequences of economic ideas from Karl Marx and capitalism. God's grand idea of the gospel has the greatest effect of all, shaping history and eternity.

Our idea of God has the greatest consequence in our life. A. W. Tozer said, "What comes into our minds when we think about God is the most important thing about us."[1] Ideas of God range from an impersonal cosmic force to a cruel taskmaster or cosmic Santa Claus to a loving heavenly Father. Each of those theological ideas leads to a different way of life, affecting everything, including the thoughts we think, the choices we make, and the actions we take.

What we believe about the Bible affects daily life in a profound way. People who believe God wrote it order their lives by it. Those who consider it only a collection of nice but nonbinding moral suggestions, or regard it as nonsense, seek guidance elsewhere.

God's Word lists what we should think about and be influenced by: "Whatever is true, whatever is noble, whatever is right, whatever is pure, whatever is lovely, whatever is admirable—if anything is excellent or praiseworthy—think about such things" (Philippians 4:8). Those ideas will reap good consequences, just as bad ideas lead to bad consequences. But let us never say that ideas have no consequences.

Divorcing Faith from Reason

Critics attack Christianity as unreasonable. Faith, they say, contradicts reason. You've heard the charges: "Faith is a blind leap in the dark"; "Faith requires one to check his brain at the door"; "Faith has been rendered meaningless in this age of scientific and intellectual enlightenment." Sadly, even some Christians divorce faith from reason. This view is neither biblically accurate nor consistent with historic, orthodox Christianity. The early Church Fathers, the Medieval Scholastics, and the Protestant Reformers believed that faith fits the biblical view of reason. As we consider the reasonableness of faith, let's remember that finite human intellect is not able to *fully* grasp infinite divine truth. But, the fact that something cannot be *fully* understood by reason does not mean it's unreasonable. Let's consider four points about the relationship between faith and reason.

First, our reasoning capacity is part of God's image in us. Human rationality reflects our Creator's rationality. Using our mind is a God-glorifying endeavor, revealing, if even dimly, His nature. The greatest commandment, recorded in the Hebrew *Shema* (Deuteronomy 6:4-5) and in Jesus' application of it (Matthew 22:37), commands us to love God with all our being, including our *minds*. We love God by pursuing truth, reasoning well, and rejecting falsehood.

Second, faith is not unreasonable. Nothing is inherently irrational about believing Jesus Christ is God's Son who died to pay for our sins. NonChristians may call it foolish (1 Corinthians 1:18), but they can't demonstrate that charge (1 Corinthians 1:25). The Protestant Reformers rationally explained the threefold nature of saving faith: (1) knowledge—of the facts of the gospel, (2) assent—to the truth of the gospel, and (3) an act of the will—to trust Christ alone for justification. We are saved by faith but the mind plays a part in that faith. We hear, process, and respond to the gospel by using our minds. Faith and reason are not and cannot be separated.

Third, the Christian faith is distinct from other kinds of faith, which are not so reasonable. Jehovah's Witnesses, Mormons, and other world religions have a type of faith, but none hold up under serious scrutiny. Christianity, however, survives the most strenuous investigation, standing on hard facts which can be rationally judged. The God of the Bible exists; He sent His Son to this world to die; and by believing in Him a person receives justification and eternal life. Faith is not a blind leap in the dark, but is supported by evidence for the biblical testimony.

Fourth, some Christian teachings are mysterious, beyond our finite understanding. Doctrines such as the Trinity (God's single essence yet threefold person-hood) and the Incarnation (two natures, one Divine, one human, in the one person of Jesus Christ) are profound mysteries. But even though not fully understood, they're not contradictions. They violate no formal laws of logic. In the final analysis, however, the Trinity and Incarnation can never be fully understood through reason. But that does not render the Christian faith irrational.

In summary, faith and reason do not compete with one another as incompatible notions. Throughout history the church has held a high view of the use of reason in the life of the saved. The Christian should use her mind to glorify God by diligently pursuing and knowing truth, by thinking clearly and properly, and by rejecting falsehood. The Christian faith is a reasonable faith, and we should value the use of reason, one of God's greatest gifts to us.

Is Truth Knowable?

During Pilate's interrogation, Jesus mentioned "truth." Pilate sarcastically replied, "What is truth?" (John 18:38). He either believed it didn't exist or that no one could know what it was. People today often say we can't know truth. Others believe we can know some truth, but not about the big things like God or morality. Both notions oppose the historic view of truth, also the Christian view, called the correspondence theory of truth. It means a statement is true if it corresponds to a fact in the world. For instance, "A bear is driving a bus" is a true statement if indeed a bear is driving a bus.

Christianity claims to describe truths about creation, history, and God's plan for humanity. Those descriptions presuppose that statements can be true—it's assumed that truth can be known. So how do we respond to people who disagree? We might ask the skeptic, "What do you *mean* by saying truth is unknowable?" He may not deny the possibility of all truth, but only truth claims about religion and God. Or, he may answer that truth is relative to people, circumstances, or times. He might, indeed, claim that all truth is unknowable. If so, we can respond along one of three avenues.

First, it cannot be true that all truth is unknowable. That claim defeats itself. The very statement sets forth a principle that it violates. For example, assertions such as: "It's impossible to write a sentence longer than three words," disprove themselves because the point of the statement is refuted by itself. If all truth is unknowable then the declared truth that all truth is unknowable could not be known. Our skeptic has refuted his own position.

Second, it can be demonstrated that some truths are known. For instance, our mythical debater's existence can be known because he must exist to say that we can't know truth. Likewise, mathematical conclusions, geographical facts, and historical events can be known with certainty. It can be confirmed that 2+2=4; that Minnesota is north of the equator; that George Washington was the first president of the United States. Such facts are known and true.

Third, many deny the knowability of truth only regarding morality and religion. We can ask, "Why do you place those subjects in a separate category? How do you justify the inconsistency of divorcing them from truth, while keeping math, science, and history in the realm of truth?" Issues about God and spiritual matters either correspond to reality or they don't, thus they are subject to inquiry like other topics. They can be investigated as can math or history, even if by different methods. Most people who say morality and religion are unknowable are just repeating a trendy phrase and have not thought through the issue.

In a culture that attacks the nature of truth, believers should be able to defend it. The viability of Christianity stands or falls upon the fundamental concept that truth exists and we can know it. Despite the theoretical nature of such discussions, we should "demolish arguments and every pretension that sets itself up against the knowledge of God, and . . . take captive every thought to make it obedient to Christ" (2 Corinthians 10:5).

Is Truth Absolute or Relative?

Modern dialogue about Christianity includes challenges unforeseen in years gone by. Tell someone you believe in something, and they might respond, "That may be true for you, but it's not true for me." This well-worn cliché reveals our culture's view of truth as relative rather than absolute. Truth is no longer considered the same for all persons, at all times, in all places. Pick your own truth; one version is as good as the next.

The relativist may argue his point by saying people once believed the world was flat, but no longer. But the truth about the earth's shape never changed. People merely traded a false belief for a true one. Or he might claim that the statement, "I feel warm," is true only for the person sensing that feeling. But it's true for all people that the person making that statement feels warmth. He may also argue that the belief that "It's cold at the North Pole" is not true everywhere, such as the equator. But it is true for everyone, everywhere, that it's cold at the North Pole.

The idea of relative truth is bankrupt for the following reasons. *First*, it defeats itself. The relativist believes the statement, "All truth is relative." But if all truth is relative, then relativism falls into that category and cannot claim to be absolutely true. Why, then, should we believe it?

Second, relativism is untenable because it entails that opposites are true. For example, some might assert that it can be true for one person that God exists, but true for another that He does not exist. Those two concepts, however, are mutually exclusive. It cannot be the case that God both exists and does not exist. Either He does or does not.

Third, the relativist view renders knowledge impossible. Gaining knowledge presupposes moving from a state of no-knowledge to a state of knowledge. If relativism is true, however, neither state truly exists, and learning is rendered impossible.

We should answer two objections aimed at absolute truth: (1) The relativist may argue that it's impossible to absolutely understand truth. But in saying that, she mixes concepts. She assumes that belief in absolute truth requires that one has an absolute understanding of truth. Those are different issues. (2) She may object that the notion of absolute truth is narrow, bigoted, or close-minded. But her belief is a narrow claim, and thus falls prey to the same criticism. She is asserting that the concept of relative truth is better than that of absolute truth. She is just as narrow-minded.

Despite the recent popularity of relativism, it lacks intellectual, philosophical, and biblical integrity. As Christians we must recognize and understand it. We swim in its waters, and should be able to refute it as we engage our culture with the gospel of Christ. The One who said, "I am the way and the *truth* and the life" (John 14:6, emphasis added), requires that we know the nature of truth and communicate it well.

Introducing Logic

Dr. Spock of *Star Trek* was portrayed as the quintessential logical thinker—precise, unemotional, a little boring. Without imitating Spock's lack of feeling or lackluster demeanor, we should strive to think logically. Part of loving God with our minds (Matthew 22:37; Mark 12:30; Luke 10:27) is logically discovering and dwelling on truth found in Scripture or His creation. C. S. Lewis once wrote that Christ wants us to have a child's heart, but a grown-up's head. That demands logic.

The foundational pillars for thinking, pursuing truth, and acquiring knowledge are the Laws of Logic. These weren't invented by Aristotle or anyone else. Like gravity, they just *are*—reflections of God's reality and the world He made. They govern the way we think, often assumed to be part of our God-given common sense. No moment goes by in which we do not use or assume logic. To deny it requires using it.

The three interconnected laws of logic are (1) *The Law of Non-Contradiction—A is not non-A.* Two contradictory statements cannot both be true at the same time and in the same respect. A person cannot talk and not talk at the same time and in the same way. (2) *The Law of Excluded Middle—Either A or non-A*. Something is either itself or not itself. It cannot be both at the same time and in the same way. Either you are reading this book or you are not. There's no middle ground. (3) *The Law of Identity—A is A*. Something is itself and not something else. God is God and not someone or something else. You are you and not someone else.

Some people contend that logic is a Western invention, having no bearing on Eastern philosophy or religion. But the laws of logic are universal, directing human thought in the Eastern mind as well as the Western mind. Those who say logic reflects only Western thought use it when they look before crossing the street. Rejecting it may lead to a quick death because either a truck is coming down the road or it's not, and they look because they know that.

Let's focus on Law #1, the law of noncontradiction—*A is not non-A*. Each time we think, we assume this law. The law of noncontradiction helps us distinguish between thoughts. When we think something, it's not something else we're thinking. To deny this law assumes it, for in denying it one is saying it's false. However, saying it's false implies a difference between truth and falsehood. But a distinction between truth and falsehood exists only because that law is true—A is not non-A.

As Christians we should be logical in our thinking, concerned with holding true rather than false beliefs, especially about our heavenly Father and what He says in Scripture. Sloppy, illogical thinking does not reflect spirituality, but the opposite. An irrational, illogical Christian reveals a lack of love for God, the basis of all logic and thinking. Being a Christian is incompatible with being illogical.

EMOTIONS

Thinking Versus Feeling

Humans feel as well as think. Because God designed us with emotions, we all know anger, joy, remorse, and other feelings. Emotions can be good, such as anger at sin, or bad, such as bitterness. As with all good things, emotions must be kept in proper context. But in much of our culture, our feelings overstep their God-intended bounds because we rank them over reason.

Emotions cannot determine truth or decide right from wrong. Feeling good does not suggest that something is true, and feeling bad does not indicate it's false. Emotions contain no content, no information by which to evaluate truth or falsehood. Our reasoning capacity performs that function. Emotions are the part of the soul that appreciates and responds to life. Expecting them to identify truth is like asking our ears to smell a flower. They can't because ears weren't made for smelling.

Mormons provide an example of depending on emotions to think. They invite people to pray over the Book of Mormon and ask God to reveal that it's true. The test for truth—emotion! The book is confirmed when the one praying is supposed to receive what they call "a burning in the bosom"—a feeling. That alleged sensation conveys Mormon sincerity but has nothing to do with the book's accuracy or lack of it. Millions of people experience sincere but contradictory emotions about their religions. Those viewpoints, however, cannot all be true because they make mutually exclusive claims about God, the universe, mankind, and salvation.

In our day, some Christians come dangerously close to this kind of spiritual operation. They believe that God speaks to them outside His Word, even using an audible voice. While this may be true, the test for authenticity should not be their feelings but agreement with God's written revelation in Scripture. Biblical, historic Christianity does not ask people to make a decision or take action based on feelings.

People often make moral decisions based on how they feel. But emotions cannot determine right or wrong any more than they can recognize truth or falsehood. According to God's Word, some things that feel good violate His standards. Gluttony and gossip may feel good, but must be evaluated by God and His Word, regardless of our feelings.

Emotions influence reason, but should not become

the key factor. When truth and falsity or rightness and wrongness are identified, feelings can and should accompany the decision. Imagine not being moved by a beautiful sunset; not marveling at the birth of your child; not feeling awe, humility, and gratitude over God's redemptive plan. Emotionless Christianity is closer to Buddhism, which teaches passionlessness. That's not what God has in mind. Christians should be passionate, but according to truth.

Jesus modeled perfect emotional balance. Saul of Tarsus pictured the opposite—a zealous Pharisee who tried to kill Christians (Acts 7:59-8:1). Like some Jews before him, his passion was not guided by truth (Romans 10:1-2). After becoming a follower of Christ, however, God redirected his emotional fervor. He channeled his passion into preaching God's Word with the same intensity as he exercised in his pre-Christian life.

Christians should follow the example of Jesus and the apostle Paul who used their emotions well by keeping them in their place. Our reasoning capacity should make decisions about both truth and morality. A mind well trained in God's Word guides us in God's way. "[His] word is a lamp to [our] feet and a light for [our] path" (Psalm 119:105).

Is Morality Relative?

"No moral standards are absolute." "That may be right for you, but not for me." "All values are cultural." These overused remarks betray our society's belief that moral values are relative. Right and wrong vary from person to person and culture to culture based on preferences, upbringing, and majority opinion. But that view is riddled with glaring problems.

First, the system is inconsistent. The relativist announces that no system is absolutely right, but then proclaims his system right and other systems—those which accept absolutes—wrong. In pronouncing the rightness of his system over others, he establishes himself as the absolute standard by which others are measured. He violates his own position by believing it.

Second, God is the standard by which everything is judged. "But just as he who called you is holy, so be holy in all you do; for it is written: 'Be holy, because I am holy'" (1 Peter 1:15-16). His moral mandates flow from His nature, and His pronouncements conform to His character. The authority to determine morals, therefore, does not fall within the jurisdiction of individuals, groups, or cultures. Those who reject God's existence or sovereignty appeal to some standard for establishing or rejecting moral values. In every system, be it moral, immoral, or amoral, something is furthest back that sets the course.

Third, moral absolutes seem unavoidable. Despite the trendy belief in moral subjectivity, certain acts are universally recognized as right or wrong. For example, all societies value honesty and condemn torturing babies. The outrage everyone feels when we hear of such atrocities exposes the innate wrongness of such heinous acts.

Fourth, relativism produces chaos. Imagine a world in which everyone lived without a sense of absolute right or wrong. No ethical standards could be imposed because there would be none. Contracts could contain lies and deception by either party. Frustrated neighbors could murder the guy next door when angered. Governments could conquer their neighbors for any reason they made up.

Fifth, justice dies under relativism. Administering justice presupposes an absolute standard. If right or wrong is based on individual determination, no statement, thought, or action could be condemned. Lying, stealing, and murder are given the green light because they're not subject to punishment. No amends could be pursued for wrongs because wrong would not exist.

Sixth, relativism tolerates monstrous cultures. No historical atrocities can be criticized. We may deplore Hitler's Germany, but it could not be labeled "wrong." If you dislike any ethnic group or you grow tired of your political opponents, exterminate them. Slavery may be different from our way of life, but it can't be called evil. If you want free labor, kidnap people and work them to death. Divorced from an ultimate, transcendent, immutable standard, such examples are inevitable.

Fortunately, few people consistently apply this belief. But this trend increasingly sways individuals, societies, and governments. Christians may, at times, be affected by it as well. But Christianity and moral relativism are incompatible. We should recognize relativism as a belief system that is intellectually bankrupt, socially unlivable, and opposed to God's Word.

PHILOSOPHY

Should Christians Do Philosophy?

When you hear the word "philosophy," do you picture an eccentric professor contemplating lofty ideas but unable to tie his shoes? Do you imagine abstract thoughts that don't matter in real life? Do you think of intellectual systems that oppose Christianity? Some philosophers are strange, and the history of ideas includes some viewpoints hostile to Christianity, but philosophy in and of itself is not Christianity's enemy.

Philosophy has been described as thinking about thinking, and all Christians should do that. The term comes from two Greek words, *philia* ("love") and *sophia* ("wisdom"), thus "loving wisdom." Nothing anti-Christian appears in that definition. Problems arise if we seek wisdom apart from God, or elevate human reason above Him, but according to Proverbs 4:5-7, God's people should love and seek wisdom.

Formal philosophy is divided into three major areas—incidentally, all core Christian issues: (1) *Meta-*

physics, which asks questions about the nature of reality: "What is real?" "Is the basic essence of the world matter, or spirit, or something else?" (2) *Epistemology*, which addresses issues concerning truth and knowledge: "What do we know?" "How do we know it?" "Why do we think it's true?" (3) *Ethics,* which considers moral problems: "What is right and wrong?" "Are moral values absolute or relative?" "What is the good life, and how do we achieve it?"

Philosophers and their thinking made our world what it is. Our society, including you and your family, is shaped by those past ideas. If we're to engage our culture with God's truth, we must study and understand that history of ideas. If we don't understand past anti-Christian thinking, we may accept its current form or be conquered by it.

Our Christian heritage embraces philosophy. Medieval scholars said, "Theology is the queen of the sciences; and philosophy is her handmaiden." Theology was most important, but her helper was philosophy. Some of the church's greatest theologians were also philosophers: Augustine, Aquinas, Ansclm, and Jonathan Edwards.

The Christian must be a philosopher to develop a worldview that makes sense and fits reality. Our philosophy should be uniquely Christian, that is, kept within the context of Christian theism. Our philosophy recognizes that God exists, that He has revealed Himself and His plan in the Bible, and that the Bible is the authority for faith and practice. If we construct a system of thought outside those bounds, we deviate from Christianity.

With respect to false teaching, we're to think well, examining truth claims so we won't be deceived by them. God gave gifts of communication to His church to spread His truth. As we think through that teaching, "we will no longer be infants, tossed back and forth by the waves, and blown here and there by every wind of teaching and by the cunning and craftiness of men in their deceitful scheming" (Ephesians 4:14). Christians must not overemphasize human reason, but philosophy, in its proper place, is a useful tool for Christians who want to prepare well to engage our world. Philosophy—thinking about thinking—is indispensable to the Christian.

The Bible Is from God

09 THE BIBLE

The Bible possesses a special quality, a divine something that people have always recognized. Written 2,000 to 3,500 years ago, it remains as relevant today as if written last night. People from all times and places have given their lives to see the Bible translated into their own language, own a personal copy, and place it into others' hands. Christians believe the Bible's special quality is its source—God. Does it really come from Him? Let's consider four lines of evidence.

First, the Bible's claims about itself: It uses the phrase "God said" fifty-four times (NIV) and similar expressions that credit it to God hundreds of times. In dozens of places it calls itself "the Word of God." That status applies to both Testaments since the author of Hebrews ranks the New Testament with the Old (Hebrews 1:1-2; 2:3), and Peter identifies Paul's writings as "Scripture" (2 Peter 3:16). The Bible clearly claims a divine origin.

Second, Jesus' view of the Bible: He called the Old Testament "the word of God" (Matthew 15:6; Mark 7:13;

John 10:35). He introduced biblical quotes with "It is written" (Matthew 4:4,7,10), the standard Jewish introduction to Scripture. In Matthew 22:43 He referred to David's words in Psalm 110:1 as spoken by the Holy Spirit. Jesus also promised that the Holy Spirit, sent by God the Father, would bring more truth, referring to the New Testament (John 14:25-26; 16:13). If the Bible is not from God, Jesus either was mistaken or He lied, a position only the most hardened skeptics hold.

Third, the Bible's unity: This collection of sixty-six books was written by about forty authors from different times and cultures. Their various personalities and experiences resulted in diverse writing styles as well as distinct forms of literature: poetry, parables, history, personal letters, and direct theological instruction. But a singular theme, God's salvation plan for mankind, runs through every page. Such unchanging focus from such a diverse background could result only from a divine source.

Fourth, the human authors' self-perception and sacrifice: Jesus was not the only authoritative person who believed in Scripture's divine origin. The prophets were convinced that they were speaking and writing God's Word. Near the end of the Old Testament era Zechariah mentions "the law [and] the words that the

LORD Almighty had sent by His Spirit through the earlier prophets" (Zechariah 7:12). Peter says in 2 Peter 1:21 that "prophecy never had its origin in the will of man, but men spoke from God as they were carried along by the Holy Spirit." Many of the prophets suffered and died for their belief that they were speaking God's Word (Matthew 23:34-35). Those men who made that claim were the only ones who really knew, and they accepted death rather than recant. Frauds and the unconvinced don't willingly submit to torture and death.

Taken together, these reasons help explain why this ancient book remains relevant today and has been translated into thousands of languages and dialects—more than any other book in history. The Bible remains the most popular book in the world. It was written by God, and it shows. Lives are changed forever by learning it and living its teaching.

How Did the Bible Originate?

Christians believe that the Bible originated from God. But what does that mean? How did He produce it, and what tools did He use? Did He just drop it from heaven or work through intermediate means? Receiving a written record of God's thoughts expressed in words requires a complex set of ingredients: human beings with language capacity for expressing ideas, physical materials to record those languages, and a coordinating process to integrate the divine and human elements.

Written language developed through several stages. The earliest form of "writing" was the drawing of objects, which developed into pictograms and logograms, pictures of things that represented sounds and nonphysical concepts. The next step was syllabic writing in which signs stood for specific sounds that could be strung together. This led to the alphabet, letters which symbolize single sounds, arrangeable in unlimited ways to communicate almost any idea, concept, or object. If it's true that one picture equals a thousand words, it's also true that a few words can verbally paint a thousand pictures.

Before paper came to biblical lands about AD 900, languages were written upon different materials that changed over time. The earliest were stones (cf. Exodus 24:12) and clay tablets, which were more or less permanent but time-consuming to write on and awkward to move. Writing much information on stone or clay was obviously impractical. A big improvement came with papyrus, made from a reed that grows in Egypt. It was light, easy to write on, and could be rolled into a scroll, but it was not durable. The parchment mentioned by Paul in 2 Timothy 4:13 was processed from animal skins. It offered improved quality and permanence, and became the most common writing material by New Testament times. Ancient writing instruments corresponded to the material written upon: chisels to engrave stone, a stylus to make impressions on clay, a reed pen for writing ink on papyrus or parchment.

Languages and physical writing materials are only tools for recording thoughts, which must originate from and be recorded by living beings. Christians contend that the ideas found in the Bible came from God, who recorded them through human authors by a process called "inspiration," meaning "God-breathed" (2 Timothy 3:16). The Holy Spirit revealed the divine thoughts and moved the human authors (2 Peter 1:21) so that they recorded the exact message of God without losing their individuality or writing style. This revealing/recording process is known as the "dual authorship" of Scripture because it incorporates both divine and human elements.

Our Bible is the result of human languages, physical materials, and human participation, all coordinated by divine oversight. It records God's exact revelation—the ideas and the words. Such a concept and process should not strike us as surprising. If God is God, He can certainly think and communicate ideas. And if He chose to reveal them, wouldn't we expect Him to arrange whatever was necessary for us to receive and record such thoughts? What we read and try to live by is the very Word of God in written form.

Missing the Cut

Many ancient writings were considered in the process of collecting the Bible into one book. Who determined the selection, and why did some books make the cut and others not? What prompted the need for such a choice, and what factors were considered? Should some of the excluded writings have been included, and if not, why not?

The central question was whether or not a book was inspired by God. But that assumes a prior issue—if God inspired any writings, wouldn't He be the one who guided the process of collecting them into His Book? The logic seems obvious, and the historic view of Christians who hold a high view of Scripture is just that—God determined the canon of Scripture; the church only discovered it. ("Canon" is a word that originally meant a reed used for measuring; then, a standard for acceptance; finally, the list of books recognized as written by God.)

In addition to the desire to know what really came from God, four developments forced the church to act:

(1) Heretics began circulating incomplete collections and obviously false writings. (2) Counterfeit books, falsely written under the name of an apostle, began to appear in some churches. (3) Christianity spread to new lands, and missionaries needed to know which sacred books to translate into new languages. (4) The edict of Diocletian (AD 303) ordered the destruction of the Christians' sacred writings and threatened death for those who refused. Believers wanted to know what books would be worth dying for.

The central factor for recognizing a book's inspiration was apostolic authorship, or at least approval, since the apostles' authority came from the Lord Himself. Specific questions used in the process included the following: (1) Was it actually written by God's prophet or apostle or someone closely associated with one? (2) Was the author confirmed by acts of God? (3) Did the book's message tell the truth about God? (4) Did the book contain God's power? (5) Was it accepted by God's people?

The process was more complex and time consuming than these few questions might suggest. But Christians then and now believe that the Holy Spirit guided the process because He was the One who inspired the writings in the first place. It would be highly unreasonable for Him to give us certain writings but then not ensure that the right ones were recognized as His.

But what of the writings that didn't make the cut, such as the Apocrypha, a collection of fourteen books of Jewish history and tradition written from the third century BC to the first century AD? The argument against including the Apocrypha in the canon includes the following: (1) The Jews never accepted it as Scripture and did not include it in their Bible. (2) What acceptance it did enjoy was only local and temporary. (3) No major church council included it in Scripture. (4) It contains errors. (5) It teaches doctrines contrary to Scripture. (6) Neither Jesus nor the New Testament quoted it even though they quoted the Old Testament hundreds of times. (7) The Christian churches that eventually accepted it, did not until many centuries later.

The divine Author of Scripture superintended the recognition of His books as much as He did their inspiration. Our Bibles contain all He inspired and nothing He didn't.

Can I Trust the Old Testament?

Preserving written documents and the accuracy of their information is no easy task, especially without modern tools like printing presses or computers. The only ancient means of duplication, hand copying, was subject to human error, and the physical materials written upon could disintegrate or be destroyed. If copies of ancient writings do survive, how can we know that what they record is what was originally written? These questions have direct bearing on the accuracy of the Old Testament, written 2,400 to 3,400 years ago.

The rules used by ancient scribes to ensure accuracy are astonishing. They were so concerned to guarantee precision that they wouldn't write even one letter from memory. Furthermore, they devised a number system to count almost everything to achieve near perfection in copying. They numbered the lines, verses, words, and letters of a book, then counted them in the copy to ensure no addition or deletion had occurred. If the count was wrong, they destroyed the copy and started over.

As a result, they were so convinced that the copy was perfect, that they considered it equal in authority to the original. The old one was usually destroyed because future physical damage might render it unreadable, leading to misunderstanding of what the text said. This process explains why so few ancient manuscripts survive today. But is there a way to confirm if these rules, even meticulously applied, resulted in accurate copies centuries later?

Our earliest complete Old Testament manuscript comes from the tenth century AD, more than a thousand years after the Old Testament was written. If we could compare our manuscripts with very ancient copies, we could verify that the scribal efforts during the intervening millennium had preserved the original text. Until 1947, no such means of comparison was available. But early that year a Bedouin shepherd boy found several large jars filled with ancient writings now known as the Dead Sea Scrolls. They contained over 500 books, including the Old Testament text from the second century BC, over a thousand years earlier than any other Old Testament manuscript. Finally, a comparison could be made.

The text of Isaiah 53 provides a remarkable example of accuracy after centuries of copying and recopying. Of the 166 words in that chapter, only seventeen letters are in question, ten of which are spelling variations. Four are minor changes of style in conjunctions. Three are from one word that does not significantly affect the meaning of the passage. The scribes did their work well. They had preserved what the prophets had written.

More confirmation of accuracy comes from comparing the Old Testament spelling of the names of twenty-six foreign kings to those kings' own documents or monuments. Our Old Testament copies from the tenth century AD accurately preserved the ancient Hebrew transliteration of the original spellings of the kings' names.

Thousands of Hebrew manuscripts and fragments reveal the painstaking efforts of the ancient scribes to pass down an accurate Old Testament text. Because of God's preserving work through those faithful scribes, we have the same Old Testament that Jesus used, the one God wrote though His prophets.

Confirming the Old Testament

History studies the past recorded in written accounts. Archaeology studies the past by finding and examining ancient objects as well as documents. One aim of archaeology is to learn of ancient civilizations outside of and often prior to written records. In the nineteenth century, critics claimed that many biblical accounts were bogus because archaeology had not verified them. But twentieth-century archaeological discoveries have repeatedly confirmed the Bible and shown the critics wrong. Let's consider some examples.

Genesis 19 records God's judgment on Sodom and Gomorrah and three nearby cities. Skeptics considered the account fictitious largely because the description sounded outrageous. After all, burning sulfur rarely rains from the sky so that the earth burns like a furnace (Genesis 19:24,28). Skeptics simply said, "No way."

But archaeological evidence tells that all five cities thrived at the time and place of the biblical account. The evidence also verifies the presence of three ingredients needed to support the Genesis story: natural petroleum products, earthquakes, and a great fire that burned with such intensity that even rocks melted together. An earthquake could have ignited the fire, exploding a subterranean oil basin, resulting in burning oil or tar raining down on the cities. No one knows exactly what happened, but the archaeological evidence harmonizes with Genesis.

In Joshua 6, the Bible records the conquest of Jericho. God gave General Joshua an unconventional strategy to say the least—march around the city for a week while occasionally blowing horns, and the enemy fortress would collapse. That plan of attack won't be promoted in books on modern military strategy. We would expect to find discrepancies between the archaeological findings and that biblical event.

But archaeology indicates the following, all consistent with Joshua's record: (1) Jericho was strongly fortified (6:5,20). (2) The siege was short (6:15), so short that people fled without taking their food supplies. (3) The city walls fell, perhaps by an earthquake (6:20). (4) The city was not plundered but was burned (6:17,24). Rather than discrepancies, we find archaeological evidence that corroborates the biblical account.

The Assyrian Empire was the big power in the eighth century BC. She conquered her world with a ferocity that was brutal even by ancient standards. Our knowledge of Assyria comes from tablets engraved during the time of King Ashurbanipal, and discoveries dating to the time of other kings: Sargon, Shalmaneser, and Sennacherib.

Once again, everything we learn from those sources confirms the Old Testament. Even the record of Sennacherib's invasion of Judah, boasting of driving people and animals from the land, avoids claiming the conquest of Jerusalem. As Isaiah promised, God had delivered the city from his hand (2 Chronicles 32:9-32).

The critics have been proven wrong repeatedly as archaeology demonstrates the accuracy of biblical passages. On the other hand, not one irrefutable archaeological finding proves Scripture wrong. The Bible's broad scope and specific details are supported by archaeological research.

Can I Trust the New Testament?

The New Testament is a collection of twenty-seven documents written by Christ's apostles and their friends 2,000 years ago. Their original writings, called autographs, no longer exist. Today we read copies of copies translated from Greek into English or other modern languages. But copyists make errors. How can we know that today's versions accurately record what the authors wrote so long ago? When we read the New Testament, is it what God intended us to have?

Scholars use two tests to evaluate a document's reliability. One is the number of ancient manuscripts that still exist. Do we have only 5 or 20 or 100 or 1000? The second test is the date of these manuscripts compared to the date of the original. Are they 100 years, 500 years, 1000 years after the original was written? The more copies we have and the closer in time they are to the original, the greater our ability to reconstruct what the original said. So let's hold a competition among ancient writings.

Aristotle taught and wrote in the fourth century BC, but we have only five copies to study, and our earliest copy is from AD 1100. That's fourteen centuries after his original. The Greek historian Herodotus wrote in the fifth century BC. But only eight copies exist today, the earliest dated AD 900, 1,300 years later. We have ten copies of Caesar's *Gallic War*, written about 50 BC. But our earliest copy is also from AD 900, almost 1,000 years after he wrote. These figures are typical for ancient writings. Investigative journalist Lee Strobel summarizes the evidence: "There is but the thinnest thread of manuscripts connecting these ancient works to the modern world."[2]

Our competition's two finalists are Homer's *Illiad* and the New Testament. The *Illiad* comes from about 800 BC, and earns second place with over 600 copies still existing. But the earliest of these is from the second century AD, a millennium after the original. Our contest winner is the New Testament. It was written in the mid- and late-first century AD. We have 5,664 Greek manuscripts or partial manuscripts. If we include Latin and other ancient languages, the number rises to 24,000. Nearly complete Greek New Testaments exist from the fourth century, only 300 years after the original. Some fragments are dated within one century, one to a mere generation, after the original. No other ancient document comes close to the New Testament.

By examining so many manuscripts that close to the autographs, scholars can reconstruct the original New Testament with amazing precision. They can determine the exact wording to 99.5 percent accuracy, less than one word per page variation. The remaining minor differences are mostly spelling discrepancies and no doctrine is affected. The New Testament we read today is reliable and therefore trustworthy. When we study it, we are learning what God intended.

Confirming the New Testament

15

THE BIBLE

Textual evidence overwhelmingly supports the New Testament's reliability, but what does archaeology say? We previously considered its confirmation of the Old Testament. Does it also corroborate the New? Let's consider three areas: the validity of Luke's material; the existence of Jesus; and the Crucifixion itself.

Luke wrote the book of Acts as a history of the early church, reporting the gospel's spread from Jerusalem to Rome. In the process he identified political figures and their offices in different governmental jurisdictions. Scholars once thought Luke invented many of those names and titles because they couldn't find them in other ancient records. But archaeology has repeatedly defended Luke. For instance, his record of Paul appearing in court before Gallio, Proconsul of Achaia (Acts 18:12-17), was rejected as unhistorical. But an inscription found at Delphi, dateable precisely to Paul's time in Corinth, names this man and his title.

Historians also rejected Luke's reference to Lysanias, tetrarch of Abilene (Luke 3:1), because they knew no other record of him. But a temple dedication has now been found that identifies him by name and title and in the right place. Luke's account has been substantiated on other details such as military units, travel routes, correlation of events to political rulers, and common phrases used only when and where Luke applied them.

Some people falsely believe that Jesus is not identified in ancient records other than the Bible. But He's mentioned by Tacitus, Suetonius, and Lucian. Tacitus was a Roman historian who lived from AD 55 to 120. In his report of Nero blaming the great fire of Rome on Christians, he refers to Christ three times. Early in the second century, Suetonius was secretary to Emperor Hadrian (AD 117-138). He writes that Claudius evicted the Jews from Rome in AD 49 because of their riots over someone called "Chrestus," corresponding to Luke's account in Acts 18:2 of how Aquila and Priscilla came to Corinth. Finally, the political humorist Lucian mockingly wrote of the crucified man Christians worshiped. He accurately described Christians' beliefs and practices as having originated with this "crucified sage."

Jesus' crucifixion may be alluded to by the decree of Claudius (AD 41-54), found in Nazareth in 1878, not to disturb graves or move dead bodies. He ordered execution for either offense. What would provoke the Emperor of the world's greatest power to require capital punishment for such a small crime? We can hardly imagine a reason unless during his investigation into the Jewish riots over "Chrestus," Claudius learned that the riots were sparked by Christians' belief in Jesus' resurrection. He wasn't about to let such "rumors" surface again and disrupt the peace. This possibility seems feasible, especially since the Jews had argued from the first that Jesus' disciples stole His body from the grave (Matthew 28:12-13).

The list of other discoveries that support the New Testament includes more geographical places, people and their titles, coins, and cultural descriptions. Not one archaeological finding contradicts the New Testament. If skeptics reject it for an alleged lack of archaeological support, consistency requires them to dismiss almost every other ancient record as well.

The Bible's "Errors and Contradictions"

All Christians have been challenged with the remark, "The Bible is full of errors and contradictions." That accusation has grown into one of the standard misconceptions of our time. Repeating it is almost a social obligation. One response for the Christian faced with this fallacy is to ask the critic to name one. Most are repeating what they've heard others say but never investigated on their own.

We should be prepared, however, for the occasional person who can cite one or more alleged biblical mistakes. And we should recognize that problem passages do exist. But so do answers, and Peter commands us to know them. "Always be prepared to give an answer to everyone who asks you to give the reason for the hope that you have" (1 Peter 3:15).

In a court of law the burden of proof lies with the accuser—one is presumed innocent until proven guilty. The same approach should dictate how we evaluate sources of information which have a long track record of being right. Claims of the Bible being proven wrong fall short of that boast. What most critics mean is that the Bible includes passages they can't figure out. So what? Christians know that better than the skeptics do.

Critics would do well to make sure they know what the text says and what it means before they question its accuracy. Many don't. (Of course, Christians are responsible to do the same.) Alleged biblical mistakes usually result from violating a principle of how to interpret literature. But before we consider some of those, what do Christians really claim about the Bible's accuracy?

We believe the inerrancy of the Bible applies only to the autographs—the original documents from the author's hand. Since copies can and do include mistakes, Christians do not claim inerrancy for them. Furthermore, translations don't always capture the exact meaning of the words and phrases in the original language. Many alleged mistakes in the Bible can be resolved by understanding better what the original text truly said.

Typical mistakes of interpretation include the following: (1) Critics may assume that what they cannot explain cannot be explained. But a hard passage does not imply a mistaken passage. (2) They often ignore or miss the context. We understand almost nothing in any text if we do that. (3) They sometimes take New Testament references to the Old as quotes when they are paraphrases or summaries. (4) They may point out number differences between accounts of the same incident, not realizing that one author may be rounding off the figures. (5) They often judge the Bible by modern, technical standards when it speaks the common language of ordinary people at the time of writing.

The Bible enjoys a much better track record than the critics. They've been proven wrong many times; Scripture, not once. Even though criticized for centuries, it has stood the test of time. But skeptics play a constructive role. Their challenges force us to study and sometimes reevaluate our interpretations. But until they improve their own game, we need not worry about their accusation that "the Bible is full of errors and contradictions." It's not.

Did Those Prophecies Come True?

Modern psychics claim to predict the future. Their supporters point to fulfilled prophecies to validate their boast. But further study reveals glaring errors, inconsistencies, and such vague predictions that almost any event might "fulfill" them. Their real success rate is about what we would expect from someone who read up on current events and simply guessed. The Bible, on the other hand, records hundreds of specific, identifiable prophecies, centuries before the anticipated outcome, and not one has failed. This remarkable batting average for biblical prophecy reveals its divine origin.

The apostles knew the Old Testament well, including its command that false prophets—anyone whose prophecy did not come true—were to be executed (Deuteronomy 18:20,22). Even with that built-in caution about prophetic issues, they believed Jesus was the fulfillment of the Old Testament Messianic prophecies. For instance, referring to Jesus, Peter proclaimed, "All the prophets testify about him that everyone who believes in him receives forgiveness of sins through his name" (Acts 10:43).

Many Bible prophecies anticipated the Messiah. Among them are His birth in Bethlehem (Micah 5:2; Matthew 2:1,4-6); His ancestry through Abraham (Genesis 12:1-3; Galatians 3:16; Matthew 1:1), the tribe of Judah (Genesis 49:10; Luke 3:23,33), and King David (2 Samuel 7:12-14; Matthew 1:1); and astounding details about His suffering, death, and burial (Isaiah 53:2-12; Matthew 26–27; Mark 15–16; Luke 22–23; John 18–19). These prophecies were very precise, given centuries before their fulfillment, and all came true. Modern psychics' predictions are usually vague, and given close enough to their alleged fulfillment that they could be anticipated, and most importantly, they usually fail.

Skeptics reject the suggestion that the Bible accurately prophesies future events. They object that Jesus deliberately altered His circumstances to give the impression He was fulfilling Messianic prophecies when He was not. But He would not be able to arrange most of the details, such as His ancestry, the place of His birth, the specifics of His death, the reactions of people around Him, or many other factors beyond His control. Nor can the fulfillment of those prophecies be dismissed as mere coincidence. They are too many and too precise. Mathematicians have calculated the odds of their coming true by chance. The likelihood is one out of a number so big it would almost stretch across this page.

Skeptics also say the books of other religions make predictions. So Christians' claim of fulfilled prophecy in the Bible is not unique. But this charge is simply not true. Other religious writings do not contain specific, verifiable, fulfilled prophecies. Their claims do not stand up under further examination.

If even one prophecy comes true, we should take notice. When hundreds come true without one failure, the Bible's uniqueness is demonstrated again. People intrigued by modern psychics should investigate the Bible's proven track record of prophecy. No other person or book compares with the Bible's detail, accuracy, and sheer number of fulfilled prophecies. The evidence is overwhelming.

What About All Those Translations?

You may have been shocked at all the translations you found the last time you went to a Christian bookstore to buy a Bible. Choosing one has become a bewildering process since the Bible has been translated into dozens of English versions as well as thousands of other languages.

The Bible has endured a lot on the road to such widespread popularity. For centuries it was written and copied one at a time on materials that decayed quickly, but it survived. It has withstood assaults by political powers from the Roman Empire to the Soviet Union who tried to eradicate it because they believed it threatened their regimes. It's been repeatedly attacked by critics wanting to discount its accuracy, but scholarly research continues to verify the biblical record. History has proven Jesus right when He said, "Heaven and earth will pass away, but my words will never pass away" (Mark 13:31).

A book might be classified a bestseller if it sells a hundred thousand copies. Sales of the Bible, however, run into the billions, including translations into more than 2,000 languages, covering more than 90 percent of the world's people. One early translation is still used today—the Septuagint, the third century BC Greek translation of the Hebrew Old Testament. Over a thousand new translations are being worked on right now, hundreds of them into new languages.

Replacement translations in the same language must also be made. One reason relates to the original language. As more manuscripts are discovered, scholars learn those ancient languages better and correct previous misunderstandings. A second reason is the changing nature of modern languages. What made sense in one generation makes less sense in the next and eventually, no sense or the wrong sense.

Translation is more complex than substituting the words of one language with those of another as some people suppose. The very structure of the languages may be completely different. Translators are guided by a translation theory, some aiming toward a more literal, word-for-word translation, others toward a dynamic-equivalent translation, rephrasing the wording to best capture the original sense. Some blend the two theories.

Picking an English translation can be confusing because many are available and more appear all the time. If possible, choose one produced by a committee of scholars from a broad spectrum of denominations and theological perspectives. That reduces unintended bias in the translation. Most Bibles include a preface that tells who translated it. Also consider who the Bible is for. An older person may understand the King James Version very well, but few teenagers will have the patience to wrestle with 400-year-old English. Also consider what the Bible will be used for: public worship, devotional reading, serious study, or something else. Different uses may require different translations.

The bottom line is that the translation should influence the life of the person using it. We read and study it to grow our souls and change our lives, and we should thank God that we live in a time and place when many good translations are available to help us on our spiritual journey.

What Is a Worldview?

Our world is teeming with diverse ideas about truth and reality. My underlying perspective differs from my neighbor next door, whose assumptions vary just as much from his neighbor across the street. One believes the answer to our problems is what the other calls evil. One person's nirvana is the next person's hell. At the heart of these diverse outlooks lies one's view of God and how that deity relates to the world. This intellectual lens through which we observe and interpret everything is called a worldview, and every person has one.

A worldview is a set of assumptions that governs our explanation of life and everything in it—a collection of core beliefs we hold without deliberately choosing them. Our worldview is the big picture that guides us through life, and, we hope, through death. This foundational frame of reference underlies our philosophy of life and our theology.

Worldviews are not intentionally constructed, but they can be analyzed. We do this by considering the answers they offer to prime questions such as: (1) What is ultimate reality? (2) What is mankind and what happens at our death? (3) What is knowledge and how do we know it? (4) What is good and how do we achieve it? (5) What is beauty and how does it relate to life? (6) Is there a basis for morality, and if so, what is it? (7) What is evil and its solution? (8) Is human history headed anywhere, and if so, where? The answers help us identify a worldview.

Some examples of worldviews are as follows: Theism believes an infinite, personal God exists and relates to the world that He created. Deism accepts a God who made the universe, but believes He's no longer involved with His creation. Atheism completely rejects belief in God. Pantheism believes the universe is God, while polytheism believes in many gods.

The word "worldview" sounds abstract, detached from everyday concerns. But understanding and distinguishing between worldviews is critically important. Every belief we hold, every issue we consider, every topic we discuss, is an extension of our worldview. Most human conflict arises from a clash between worldviews. Whether we consciously think of it or not, our worldview permeates our lives, determining our values and grounding our life compass. Our thoughts and choices are filtered through our worldview, and our actions reflect it.

The practical consequences of worldviews can be seen across the spectrum of human life from individual tragedies to global catastrophe. A lonely sixteen-year-old who accepts a worldview of despair and hopelessness takes drugs and ruins her future. Karl Marx, Vladimir Lenin, and Joseph Stalin shared a worldview that resulted in the slaughter of tens of millions and wrecked human civilization in much of the world.

Everyone benefits from exploring, discovering, understanding, and being able to articulate his own worldview. But it's even more essential for the Christian if he's to serve and honor God to the maximum. Believers can use awareness of other worldviews as common ground with unbelievers—a springboard to dialogue about the gospel of Jesus Christ. Worldviews matter very much, and we as Christians should know our own and be familiar with others as well.

One Infinite, Personal God

Western society was based for centuries on the belief that God created the world, revealed Himself to it, and intervened in its affairs. But the cultural awakening called the Renaissance and the resurgence of critical thinking known as the Enlightenment challenged the old assumptions. Mankind's rationalism rather than God's revelation became the authority for truth, and modernism was born. This shift in intellectual gravity was the epicenter of a transition in dominant worldviews.

The old worldview, which guided the West for centuries, is called theism. Theism believes that one infinite, personal God is the ultimate reality. As stated above, this God created the universe, disclosed Himself to mankind, and gets involved with this world and us, unprompted by any force outside Himself. He is transcendent over the world and immanent (currently present and active) within it.

Three major religions are theistic: Judaism, Islam, and Christianity. The first two are purely monotheistic—believing in only one Person of God. Christianity believes in a tri-personal God—a Trinity—three centers of personal consciousness interacting in one monotheistic union. Let's explore in more depth the basic beliefs of Christian theism, divided into three sections.

1. Beliefs About God and the World: God is infinite rather than limited, and personal rather than a mere cosmic force. He created the world from nothing—it's neither fashioned from preexisting materials nor emanates from His essence. Since nothing preexisted Him or coexisted with Him, the universe is not eternal. While He designed the world to operate by laws He created (providence), He retains the right and power to intervene directly into the world's affairs (miracles). Thus God is transcendent—existing beyond the world—and immanent—actively sustaining the universe and operating within it.

2. Beliefs About Mankind and Morality: God created mankind in His own image as a personal being with whom He could relate. God's holy character is reflected in universal, absolute moral standards that apply to all humans. Mankind was created good but with the freedom to choose for or against God's holy will. Christian theism believes mankind fell through Adam's sin, passed down to all of us. God gives us certain rights but holds us accountable to fulfill responsibilities.

3. Beliefs About History and Eternity: History is linear—a sequence of events aimed at God's purposes. It develops through God's sovereign oversight usually implemented through the agency of mankind's decisions and actions. Like history, each life develops toward a goal. Individual destiny results in reward or punishment based on one's relationship to God. History and each human life are therefore meaningful, possessing eternal significance.

The existence of an infinite, personal God is the pivotal teaching of theism. Based on His character, theism provides three critical human functions: rational thought, personal relationships with God and people, and an ethical life. A true Christian theist recognizes the claim this worldview makes on its adherents—living each moment to the glory of the Triune God who is really there.

Many Finite Gods

Polytheism is the belief in many finite, personal gods who rule distinct realms of the universe, such as the gods of ancient Greek, Roman, and Norse mythologies. Greek and Roman cultures remained polytheistic until Christian theism rose to supremacy. But as Christianity's influence has waned in the West, polytheism has resurfaced.

Polytheistic systems vary. Some portray the gods as equals, each ruling his or her own realm. Others rank the gods in a hierarchy, perhaps with one top god, such as Zeus in ancient Greek mythology. This type of polytheism is called henotheism. The number of gods may also differ—some systems containing a set amount, others an indefinite number of gods.

The Old Testament teaches one unique God (Deuteronomy 6:4). Thus ancient Israel was a monotheistic island in a sea of polytheistic peoples—the Babylonians, Assyrians, Egyptians, and other inhabitants of Palestine. The New Testament stresses the same: "There is but one God, the Father, from whom all things

21 WORLDVIEWS

came and for whom we live" (1 Corinthians 8:6). Early church apologists argued against the polytheism of the Roman Empire, largely adopted from the earlier Greeks, claiming that the universe was ruled by one unique, eternal, invisible, unchanging God.

Despite the variations among polytheistic systems, the following views are common. Multiple, finite gods oversee parts of the world, often contending with one another when their interests clash. The world is thus an arena of chaotic competition more than a unified system, as the word "universe" suggests. Nature, not the gods, is eternal, and the natural world gives birth to the gods. The gods are therefore immanent (present) within the world, but not transcendent over it.

The gods live out their competition in the realm of humanity, even including sexual encounters between gods and humans in some classical mythologies. As a direct consequence of no ultimate god, values and morality are relative, although limited moral dictates may be issued by the gods. Evil may be viewed as intrinsic within nature, sometimes an outgrowth of the gods' initial conflict among themselves.

As a rational worldview polytheism fails in several areas. Ultimate reality, if it is truly ultimate, cannot contain multiple, competing divine beings. Because there cannot be multiple ultimates, "many gods," by definition, must be limited. If the gods are not eternal and infinite, why worship them? Eternal nature, out of which the gods arose, would be more worthy of worship, as in pantheism. Nature is closer to being ultimate than is its offspring. But science clearly points to a beginning for nature. So it cannot be ultimate. Furthermore, since the gods of polytheism reflect human weaknesses and shortcomings, why would we revere them? This worldview seems to be the product of human imagination more than a reflection upon reality.

Whether expressed in terms of revitalized paganism, or New Age beliefs, or Mormonism, polytheism does not fit the evidence. More consistent with Scripture, science, and life experience is the belief that one ultimate God precedes, created, and sustains everything else.

All Is God

In recent decades Eastern religions have invaded the West, bringing their worldview of pantheism in tow. Whether in direct religious teaching as in some forms of Hinduism and Buddhism, or infused into New Age spiritualities, or expressed in popular media such as "The Force" of the *Star Wars* movies, pantheistic leanings saturate Western society.

Pantheism comes from Greek words meaning "all" and "God," and that's what it means. God is everything; everything is God; all is one. God and the world are synonymous. Ultimately everything is one infinite, impersonal reality. Apparent distinctions between things are an illusion. God did not create the world; it emanates from Him—an extension of Himself like light from the sun.

Since all is one, you and I are also God. Union with Him is the goal of each person. Our challenge is to receive enlightenment, that is, to realize that all is one and experience that oneness. Since God is beyond distinctions of good and evil, union with Him requires moral transcendence—becoming dispassionate or detached from moral laws. Therefore, morality is temporary and relative, not founded upon any absolute. Evil is an illusion like everything else, eventually to be reunited with the One.

Individual destiny is resolved by the repeated cycle of life called *karma*. One's current status as a human, or a goat, or a bug is determined by actions in a previous life. Death ends individual, personal consciousness, but the impersonal soul is reincarnated into the next life. Centuries of reincarnation are necessary to work off the bad karma of previous lives to remerge with the One. History is therefore cyclical rather than moving toward a goal, but eventually everything will be reunited as one.

Pantheism suffers four weaknesses related to reason, reality, the human self, and morality. (1) Its claim that reason cannot offer information about God uses reason to do just that. And reason requires distinctions between concepts, a distinction that does not exist according to pantheism. (2) How does the pantheist separate reality and illusion? If the apparent reality is not real, why bother to deny it? And if reality is only an illusion, the illusion is a real illusion; so there are two realities rather than one. (3) If the pantheist says he's not real, he refutes his own view because someone real is making that statement. Also, if God is the unchanging reality and I am God, I cannot change. But according to pantheism I must change through reincarnation to become enlightened about my deity. (4) Despite pantheism's claims of transcendence over moral ideals, the law of karma abounds with moral connotations.

The Bible teaches that God created the world from nothing—it is neither God nor an emanation from Him. The Christian Scriptures always maintain the distinction between Creator and creation. Pantheists do exactly what Paul warned of in Romans 1:25, "They exchanged the truth of God for a lie, and worshiped and served created things rather than the Creator."

All Is in God

When we look at each other, we see our bodies. But the real you or me, the soul, indwells and animates the body. Could that human design be a model of God and the world? Is God a cosmic spirit, inhabiting the universe like a soul in a body? Some people think so. That worldview is called panentheism. *Pantheism* means "all is God." God and the universe are the same. He's no more or less than the universe. *Panentheism* means "all is *in* God." The universe is included in Him, but He's more than the universe—as you are in your body, but are more than just your body.

The panentheist's God is very different from the God of theism. As the world changes, God changes. In other words, He evolves with the universe. He's described as having two aspects. One is His reality—what He actually is; the other is His potential—what He might become. God did not create the universe, but works with it to develop it into what it and He could be. He doesn't directly intervene in the world's affairs, but coaxes it along the path He desires. He thus guides, but does not control, the world's and His own evolution.

Since you and I are part of the universe, we're some of what God has evolved into. Our purpose is to add to His happiness by helping Him become what He wants to be. Moral values are based in God's essence, but since He's always changing, morality also changes. History is a random process without beginning or end, and even God does not know the future. When you and I die, we won't know conscious existence, but will be a mere memory in the mind of God.

Inconsistencies make panentheism hard to accept. Consider two: (1) How did the process start? If God's potential preceded His reality, how did anything become real from mere potential? On the other hand, what is real cannot precede its potential to be real. So we're faced with a cosmic chicken and egg dilemma unless the panentheist wants to introduce a God behind his own God. (2) How do we know anything is changing without a constant by which to measure the change? When we fly at night within the clouds, unable to see the moon, stars, or lights on the ground, we see no movement. We sense it only if we have a fixed reference point by which to mark our progress. Without that unchanging reference point we cannot know that God or the universe is changing. The panentheist is thus unable to know his own system.

The God of Christian theism is perfect and thus unchanging, distinct from the world He created. God's providence rules creation rather than evolves with it. We please God by living a holy life, but we don't help Him become something He's not. Paul reminded the Athenian philosophers that "[God] is not served by human hands, as if he needed anything, because he himself gives all men life and breath and everything else" (Acts 17:25).

God Turned Away

After the Reformation, many thinkers challenged more than Rome's abuses. Theism's revelation through the Word gave way to belief in our own sufficiency. Mankind's mind subverted the need for God to tell us His ways, and theism found itself on hard times. The main beneficiary of theism's decline was deism—belief in a Creator who abandoned His world.

Deism accepts theism's view that God created the world. But in deism's view, He then turned His back, unconcerned and uninvolved, no longer engaged with the world He made. God set the cosmos to run by natural law and let it be. No miracles occur because He won't interfere. Deists believe in God's total transcendence over the universe, thus He lacks any immanence—He is not present within it. He made the world like a giant clock, wound up and left to run on its own. The universe is a closed system of uniform cause and effect—natural law is inviolable—thus no miracle is possible or needed.

In this view, we have no connection to our Maker. As a mere First Cause, God does not concern Himself with our redemptive need. We're part of the clockwork universe, left on our own to fend for ourselves. We possess intelligence, creative capacity, and freedom, all unrelated to God. Some deists believe in a generic moral code, grounded in the law of nature. What evil there is comes from assault on our reason, but since reason varies, values and virtues aren't absolute. For other deists, whatever *is* is right, thus no basis for ethics is found at all. Evil and good cannot be distinguished, so right and wrong do not exist.

Deists differ on their views of history and eternity. Most believe history is linear and purposeful but not very important because God remains outside it. Most think mankind lives on after death but their views of the afterlife vary. Those who think God implanted a moral code in nature believe we'll be judged for our choices in life. Others conclude that judgment implies divine intervention into our world, which they don't allow, thus no judgment comes.

Deism suffers several problems: (1) It starts with an inconsistency, rejecting miracles but accepting the biggest miracle of all—creation of the world from nothing. So the claim that God performs no miracles lacks credibility. If He performed that first momentous act, why not others? (2) If no revelation from God is given other than what we see of Him in the universe, how do we know it's a clockwork system throughout? We've not been everywhere to be able to draw that conclusion. The truth is, we don't know, and thus deism disqualifies itself as a viable worldview. (3) Modern science has demonstrated that the universe is not the mechanical, clockwork system upon which deism was built. So-called absolute natural laws are not absolute after all.

Sadly, many Christians live as if deism were true, as though God is distant, detached from them and their needs. But the living God is "not far from each one of us" (Acts 17:27); He is eager to help in our time of need. By living with that dependence, we proclaim our belief in a living God who cares for us.

No God at All

Atheism is uncommon but influential—an underlying assumption in science, psychology, education, and other fields. Many people may doubt God's existence (agnosticism), while few deny belief in a God of some kind. But those who do, confess their faith that the world is all there is. Astronomer Carl Sagan became famous for saying, "The cosmos is all there is, or ever was, or ever will be." The distinction between the atheist and those who merely question God's existence is that the atheist dogmatically asserts that he *knows* there is no God.

Many atheists believe the universe is eternal. Others think it began from nothing and without cause—a random accident. Either way, since the universe is all there is, it is self-sustaining, not needing the aid of a supernatural being. According to atheism, we created God in our minds. So-called evidence for God is wishful thinking, a projection of our need.

A man is a mortal being, made only of physical molecules—just a body with no soul or spirit. Universal moral laws imply a Lawgiver, so no such laws are

25 WORLDVIEWS

allowed. In the absence of God, ethical values are of our own making, and relative to the situation. So morality is whatever we do to get what we want. Most atheists point to evil as proof of God's nonexistence. Evil comes from our ignorance; thus the only possible answer must be found in education.

A human being's duration covers only the years of this life. When I die, I am no more—not in heaven, or hell, or anywhere. Some atheists dream of a corporate immortality of our species, hoping for a future utopia for the human race. Our collective reasoning, applied through science, can create this heaven on earth for posterity.

Atheism cannot overcome several major hurdles: *First,* it cannot be confirmed. No one can prove the nonexistence of something that does not exist. I cannot verify that there is no Atlantis. Unless I examine every site where Atlantis might be or might have been and discover it's not there, I cannot say with certainty there's no Atlantis. Unless the atheist explores every possible avenue to prove there's no God, her search can't draw that conclusion.

Second, it cannot be lived. All atheists hold certain values, but without a God behind the universe, our lives are merely the product of chance and time. No true values result from such cosmic chaos. But the atheist illogically lives by some set of values.

Third, it does not adequately explain evil. The atheist recognizes evil, but cannot identify its source or address the problem other than point to ourselves. He can't really construe why it's there or suggest what to do about it. He's caught by the fact that evil assumes a standard of non-evil by which to classify evil as it is. But without a final standard of good (God), atheism removes its basis for admitting evil.

The atheist neither proves his case nor lives consistently with it. He reveals his inconsistency by holding to many of the values of theism but with no basis for doing so. The position is irrational and unlivable as the Bible says pointedly in Psalm 53:1, "The fool says in his heart, 'There is no God.'"

I Don't Know About God

In Acts 17, the Epicurean and Stoic scholars of Athens, the intellectual center of the ancient world, escorted the apostle Paul to their meeting and asked what he'd been preaching in the market. He began his oration by citing the inscription on an altar that read, "TO AN UNKNOWN GOD" (Acts 17:23). Based on that confession of ignorance, Paul explained Christian theism and the truth of the living God.

The Greek word from which "unknown" is translated is the word from which we get "agnostic." The word for "knowledge," *gnosis*, gave its name to an ancient belief system called "gnosticism," because they claimed special knowledge. By adding the negative prefix "a" we derive "agnosticism," meaning "no knowledge." Agnosticism is the worldview that says we cannot know if God exists.

The "soft" variety of agnosticism says we *don't* know if God exists. The "hard" version asserts we *can't* know if He exists. The soft agnostic modestly admits, "I don't know if there's a God." The hard agnostic aggressively challenges others: "I don't know if there's a God, and you don't either!" Almost everyone in hard times might qualify as a soft agnostic: "Where is God in the midst of my suffering?" We'll concern ourselves with the hard version, the committed worldview that no one can know if God exists—He's completely unknowable.

Hard agnosticism originated with the eighteenth-century philosopher Immanuel Kant, who believed that reality existed, but we couldn't know it. Reality and our ability to perceive it are separated by a vast gulf. We can know that reality exists, but we cannot know what it is. All we can know is how it appears to us, its image, not what it is in itself.

The Christian has little argument with the soft agnostic who merely confesses inability to know enough about God to decide if He's there or not. He leaves the door open for future knowledge, which the wise Christian gently provides. Hard agnosticism, on the other hand, is flawed from the start. One cannot distinguish between reality's image and reality itself unless one knows something of both. No comparison can be made unless one has some knowledge of the things being compared.

Hard agnosticism defeats itself by an internal inconsistency—claiming to know something of what it declares is unknowable. If reality is unknowable, how does the agnostic know that? If you claim that you don't know anything, you are claiming knowledge of that. And if you can know one thing, you're not really an agnostic. Furthermore, asserting that God's existence cannot be known presumes certain knowledge about Him, which is unknowable according to agnosticism.

Following Paul at Athens, we can fill the gap in people's admission of ignorance. The Holy Spirit supplied knowledge of God through the prophets and apostles, recorded in Scripture. And by His ongoing work in the hearts of men and women today, He enables people to understand the truth we offer. Even the most committed agnostic can come to God by the enabling grace of Him "who wants all men to be saved and to come to a knowledge of the truth" (1 Timothy 2:4).

Just Choose and Act

The twentieth century inflicted horrors upon humanity beyond any in previous history. Almost as bad as mass atrocity was the despair that gripped mankind's collective soul in a post-theistic world. Removing God from the realm of reality left us to create and escape catastrophes of our own making. Corporately and individually we now ask "Who are we?" in the midst of this mess, and we find no answer.

Nineteenth-century Danish philosopher Søren Kierkegaard rejected the notion of believing based on logical reasoning and objective facts, concluding that we must simply make a leap of faith. German philosopher Friedrich Nietzsche soon proclaimed that God was dead, morality was mankind's invention, and the "will to power" (his almost pantheistic phrase for the impersonal will of all that is) mattered most. Nothing of value exists. In the wake of two World Wars and the regimes of Hitler and Stalin, millions concluded that life was absurd and mankind meaningless.

The soil was prepared for existentialism—an applied

philosophy of atheism more than its own worldview. (A theistic form of existentialism exists, but our focus will be the atheistic version.) It stresses human freedom, the absurdity of life, and our responsibility to define ourselves through choice and action. We thus create our own reality. In the fifties and sixties the existential writings of Jean Paul Sartre and Albert Camus influenced Western universities with this view that life is absurd. We can validate our existence and minimize despair only by making choices. Thus, exerting choice, sometimes called "freedom," became the premier value.

According to existentialism, God does not exist. The material universe is all there is. In the absence of God and His providence, we create our own hope and love by the exercise of our will. I create my future, my world, my morality by using my freedom to choose. I create value by revolting against the absurdity of the world around me. But I must do this authentically rather than follow the crowd. Since there's no transcendent Lawgiver, ethics are related to mankind alone. Whatever I choose is what is good. History is a series of events without meaning or purpose. At death we cease to exist, but we should courageously face this inescapable end.

Existentialism falls short at its critical point of finding a reason to live in this rotten world. It provides no basis for choosing one action over another. If value is created by one's choice, how can I think my choice is better than Charles Manson's? Furthermore, if some basis could be found for preferring my good over Manson's, does that good have any meaning? Rather than finding a way out of an absurd world, existentialism compounds the problem.

For the existentialist it really makes no difference if one imitates Hitler or Mother Teresa as long as it is one's authentic choice. When we die, it's all over, so who really cares? But if we survive death, as the Bible teaches, what we choose and do in this life has eternal significance. Christians can face death with confidence because Jesus' death "free[d] those who all their lives were held in slavery by their fear of death" (Hebrews 2:15).

We're Number 1

The Westminster Shorter Catechism proclaims that the chief end of man is to glorify God and enjoy Him forever. The humanist view, on the other hand, honors mankind as God and praises ourselves above all else. Humanism is a form of atheism that elevates us and our achievements to the supreme position in the universe. (Humanism appears in both Christian and secular forms, but we'll focus on the latter.) As the most exalted reality, humanity lives for its own purposes rather than to serve God or any other transcendent aim. Everything else exists for us. The most noble life is pursuing our own interests, accomplishments, and happiness.

During the Middles Ages, Western interpretations of reality placed God at the center of all things—a theocentric universe. But as Renaissance thinkers explored Classical literature and philosophy, they shifted the emphasis to humanity and our ability to reason apart from divine revelation—an anthropocentric universe. We thus looked within ourselves rather than to God to discover truth and to solve life's problems. The foundation of humanism was laid, although the term arrived later.

Almost all humanists deny God's reality, certainly His role as Creator. As committed naturalists, they believe the universe is self-existing and self-sustaining. Mankind has emerged from an evolutionary process that brought the universe and us to our current state. As the name "humanism" implies, man is the measure of all things, and the highest reality is found in us.

Since human nature is flexible and neither good nor bad, we can shape it to our liking. Individuals and society are moldable, waiting to be transformed to produce society's common good. The attainment of our potential is the highest goal. Since no God or other absolute exists, no divine consent is available or needed for ethics or morality. All standards and values are subject to change depending on circumstances.

By reason alone we identify problems and create solutions. Individuals don't survive death, but our collective ingenuity in life can design and direct our corporate future. Well-educated human rationality rather than divine aid will lead us to our desired destiny.

But several major questions remain unanswered by humanist ideals. For instance, what elite group determines the common good for the rest of us? Who selects the direction of our evolution? How can some human traits be considered undesirable and deliberately evolved out of our current makeup if the only standard of good and bad is fluctuating social consciousness? Decades of social engineering through education have not altered the fundamental nature of humanity. Indeed some see increased antisocial behavior as a result of human-based education.

Humanists have replaced the infinite, personal God of the Bible with themselves. But humanity as god lacks a basis by which society can allege that the corporate "good" it selects is better than history's most evil regimes. Faith in human reason and education cannot duplicate the inner transformation wrought by the Spirit of God. His revelation through Christ and Scripture provides a transcultural foundation for the values humanists seek.

Economics Rules

Since the early 1990s Marxist governments have become less numerous. During the twentieth century, Marxist theory traveled around the globe, spreading revolution wherever it went. Marxist philosophy, a form of atheist materialism applied to economics, believes history is determined by the struggle between social classes.

The name comes from Karl Marx (1818-1883), a German thinker born into a Jewish family that converted to Christianity when he was a boy. Initially serious about Christianity, his spiritual passion faded, and Marx became an atheist before college. After being exiled from Germany for radical political activities, he traveled to Paris, then settled in London. He spent the rest of his life studying and writing, publishing his *Communist Manifesto* in 1848 (along with Frederick Engels, whom he met in Paris) and *Capital* in 1867.

Marx rejected any notion of a Creator or transcendent being. The universe started and sustains itself— no outside force required. We created God and religion in our image to meet our needs. Matter is the highest reality—evolved into mankind as its most elevated form.

Since no transcendent Lawgiver exists, Marxism rejects moral absolutes. It considers mankind good, but believes in evil, described as economic inequity and the ensuing abuse of power. Human injustice results from class conflict between the haves and have-nots. Private property amplifies greed, leading to social ills, which must be corrected by revolution replacing the old economic structures with new ones. The ends justify the means as long as those means promote the communist society Marxism seeks.

Marxists maintain a clear goal for history that is predictable according to set economic laws. Human suffering will be eliminated by creating an ideal society. Capitalism will grow, increasing the wealth of property owners and the number of poor workers, until the latter revolt and institute communism. This new society will have no wages, money, or social classes, and eventually no state. Utopia results.

Marxism falls short on several counts:

1. Individuals and society are more than economic. To suggest that a change of economic order can lead to an ideal world is a naive, simplistic response to complex problems.

2. The Marxist record of dismal failures speaks for itself. The nearly universal breakdown of Marxism throughout the world since the early 1990s led to its collapse as a viable theory. It has been repeatedly tried, but simply does not work.

3. Marxism does not fulfill the human need it promises to meet. People under communism generally don't find it liberating and satisfying but oppressive and intolerable. The so-called classless society of the former Soviet Union, for instance, included two classes: the ruling elite and the masses. The first controlled life with an iron fist and brutalized the other. Wherever Marxism has been tried, its path is strewn with illegal arrests, forced labor camps, torture, and mass executions.

The dream of an ideal society is admirable, and Christians believe one will come. But the true revolution is in the human heart, not in the streets. Utopia won't result from communist tanks rolling over defenseless countries, but when Christ returns to rule with truth and justice.

They're All the Same

A truly pluralistic society allows all views, especially in its educational institutions. Many worldviews are presented to students from which they can choose without bias. But finding such a free-thinking society has proven no easy task. Our version of pluralism boasts of such tolerance, but violates its claim. For instance, when a Christian presents her position she is often shouted down as an arrogant bigot. Our pluralistic society won't tolerate her.

Pluralism can be understood in two ways. At one level, it means multiple worldview and religious options from which to choose. That is true—we live in a pluralistic world. But pluralism has evolved into its own worldview—the belief that all religions and worldviews are equally correct. Thus, any religious claim to exclusive truth is incorrect. But, in the process, pluralism itself claims to be the exclusive truth.

Religious pluralism assumes what it wants to prove—that all religions are equally safe paths to God, nirvana, or whatever their form of final destiny. In effect, it says that no religion that claims to be the only way is true. But the pluralist himself is making an exclusive truth claim when he says all religions lead to God.

Pluralism also affects ethics, rejecting any notion of universal moral principles. All values must be regarded as equal, thus none are binding. To be consistent, the pluralist must agree that the results of Nazism, Buddhism, Christianity, or even cannibalism, are equally worthwhile. Pluralism fails in part because it must condone the outcome of all worldviews, even the most barbaric, to be consistent with itself. Even if someone could truly believe such a claim, that doesn't address the truth question of any worldview. Finding a moral Buddhist or Christian does not prove Buddhism or Christianity true. We find moral and immoral adherents in all religions.

As hinted above, the irony of pluralism is its own intolerance. Any view that does not espouse pluralism is rejected and ridiculed. People who have been attacked by the politically correct movement, especially on university campuses, know the shocking degree of intolerance at the heart of pluralism. A further irony is that pluralists really don't view all other positions as equal. They don't actually consider Hitler's views on par with Churchill's or Roosevelt's.

The errors of the pluralist worldview are obvious: (1) The hypocrisy exposed by its own intolerance. This can be seen in the pluralist's hostility toward religions that claim exclusive truth. (2) The violation of logic. Two views that affirm and deny the same point in the same way at the same time cannot both be true. For instance, Jesus and Muhammad cannot both be the only, final source of God's truth. (3) The rejection of the possibility of truth. The starting assumption of pluralism is that no absolute truth exists. (4) The destruction of any basis for morality. Taken to its logical conclusion, this leads to chaos and social destruction.

Pluralism does not achieve what it says it wants—open dialogue on all positions. It stifles all views other than itself. The university and the culture would benefit from returning to genuine tolerance of diverse ideas. The Christian can set the tone by presenting his worldview with grace and respect, inviting discussion of other positions, and preparing well to engage the issues.

The Anti-Worldview

A revolution in thinking known as *the Enlightenment* engulfed seventeenth and eighteenth-century Europe. The way Westerners thought for the previous thousand years changed. Human reason and natural science replaced religion as the recognized authority. That new age became known as *modernism*. During the final third of the twentieth century, the West began undergoing another intellectual revolution when a denial of Enlightenment principles spread from universities to the broader culture. *Postmodernism* is the term used to identify this new worldview, which might be called an *anti-worldview* because it rejects all worldviews.

The worldview of postmodernism is still taking shape. Since this new way of thinking (and living) is evolving, it may take generations for a recognized definition to be accepted, but certain traits are detectable. Postmodernism emphasizes experience more than facts, desires symbols more than logic or science, and integrates reason with faith. We'll briefly consider two applications of postmodernism: linguistic and sociological.

31 WORLDVIEWS

Postmodernism affects how we use and interpret language, especially written texts. It points out the inner bias of all communicators since all are influenced by their own experience and perspective. No one is completely objective. As postmodern awareness spreads, speakers and authors may alter how they portray their ideas. They will likely convey "truth" through artistic images and literary flow rather than bare facts. Persuasion may be achieved more through beauty than debate. Ideas might be embedded within a story as opposed to a logical argument.

The sociological application of postmodernism can reveal its darker side. Since no objective meaning exists, language doesn't record meaning, but only expresses an agenda. Postmodernism can be used to discount all interpretations of reality as biased products of various cultures, none more credible than another. The idea of universal truth is merely a means of oppression. Social divisions of race, class, and gender compete for power, each group trying to impose its "truth" on the others. So the accuracy of differing viewpoints is not important; "tolerance" is. Interpretation has little to do with grasping the author's intent, but is about probing the power struggle in the community where she wrote. So when reading a text, we don't discover meaning but make our own as we guess what social factors were behind the writing. This new method of interpreting is called *deconstructionism*.

The negative form of postmodernism includes an internal contradiction. If it's true, then its main point—the rejection of universal truth—is wrong, because it's true. To be consistent, postmodernism must be seen as just another interpretation, no more viable than the others. Consider the possible irony: Some "postmodern" people try to convince us that their view is right (an internal contradiction), but use enlightenment tools of logic and language, reason and rationality to do so.

Despite the risks associated with postmodernism, it offers the (modern) world an open door for rethinking Christianity. The old, modernist reasons for rejecting Christ are abandoned by the postmodernist. Therefore a new willingness to reexamine biblical faith may accompany the spread of the postmodernist perspective. As a result, Christians may find increased opportunity to communicate the gospel story, including the use of postmodern methods. If postmodernism truly develops in a more open way, as its proponents claim it is, the Christian message may be included more, and believers may be allowed to shape the new era.

Does God Exist?

"Does God exist?" is the ultimate question. But "Does God exist?" is a different question than "Can we prove that God exists?" Nothing, including God, can be proven or disproven in a final, absolute sense.

Scientific research is the current, preferred method of investigation. The scientific method investigates by repeating, observing, and measuring. But nonmaterial concepts are not repeatable, observable, or measurable. So the scientific method cannot examine historical, philosophical, moral, or religious knowledge. Thus, God's existence or lack of it cannot even be probed by the scientific method, let alone proven or disproven.

The same is true for Alexander the Great, because history is nonrepeatable. We have considerable evidence that he existed, but we cannot prove it beyond any possible doubt. Human emotions are also not observable or measurable. The smile on a parent's face at the birth of a child can be seen, but the joy itself cannot. So, belief or disbelief in God, like belief or disbelief in Alexander or human emotions, must be based on evidence or lack of evidence, not proof.

Evidence for God's existence divides into three categories. The first is Scripture. God's existence is revealed from the Bible's first verse, "In the beginning God created the heavens and the earth" (Genesis 1:1). His existence and active presence saturate the remaining sixty-six books. Since the Christian accepts the Bible as true, sufficient evidence is found in its pages.

The second category of evidence is found within nature, including mankind's nature. Romans 1:20 tells us that God's invisible qualities are seen in God's creation. Psalm 19:1 states, "The heavens declare the glory of God." The intricate, complex, purposeful design of human beings, more than any other created thing, reveals an intelligent designer. Created in God's image, all humans sense God's reality. Romans 2:14-15 indicates that the inner sense of God is known even among people without God's written revelation in Scripture.

A third category of evidence is offered by the logical arguments of philosophy. God's existence is the only reasonable answer to several big questions. Question 1: How did the universe originate? Everything that begins has a cause. The laws of physics reveal that the universe had a beginning, thus it must have had an initial, uncaused cause. That first cause is God.

Question 2: How can the universe be complex and yet ordered? Science informs us that life cannot exist without the exact order of the world as it is. This precise, life-sustaining design suggests a purposeful designer—God. If you or I found a computer in a desert, we would conclude that someone had designed it rather than it spontaneously developing out of the sand. The universe is vastly more complex than a computer. Believing it developed spontaneously out of nothing requires more faith than believing in God.

Question 3: Why do all cultures hold to objective moral values? Some of the particular values vary, but every culture senses right and wrong and expects justice to be upheld. The universal standards of objective moral values and justice points to a final standard—God.

When all the available evidence is considered, it overwhelmingly supports the existence of a personal, moral Spirit distinct from the world but active in it. God exists and knowledge of Him is possible. Honest, objective investigation repays our efforts with more than adequate evidence to know Him.

Who Made God?

Made in God's image, children begin to ponder their Maker while very young, long before they grasp ideas like eternity or self-existence. A child might ask, "Who made God?" The question reveals the child's natural curiosity and a childlike assumption—that God had a beginning. But God is self-existent, not depending on anything for His being. He is ultimate, the farthest thing back. Theologians call this *aseity*, from a Latin word meaning "of oneself."

Before we consider the issues, two critical distinctions should be noted: (1) Christians don't claim that whatever *is* was caused, but that whatever *began* was caused. (2) Christians don't believe that God is self-caused, but uncaused.

Consider four brief arguments supporting an uncaused God, a God without beginning.

1. The Argument from Science: Before modern science, some philosophers thought the world was eternal, uncaused. No explanation of its origin was needed. But in that way of thinking, why can't God be uncaused as

33

GOD

well? On the other hand, if the universe is caused, as modern science testifies, what or Who caused it? Such a question suggests the possibility of a Designer behind the world. Either way, God, the originator of everything else, is not out of the question.

2. Examples of Uncaused Things: Some people may object that nothing exists without a cause. But consider mathematical truths: $2 + 2 = 4$ wasn't caused; it just is. If the skeptic admits that truth in math, why not of God?

3. The Skeptic's Logical Error: She alleges that everything, including God, if there is One, has a cause. But she commits a logical error. She assumes the conclusion she's investigating, called "begging the question." God needs a cause only if one assumes that *everything* needs a cause. But if only things that *began*, finite things, need a cause, God can be the uncaused Source of everything else.

4. The Limited Options: Only three alternatives exist: everything must be caused, self-caused, or uncaused. God cannot be option one—caused—because whatever is farthest back is God. If what we call "God" is caused, then whatever caused Him must be God. Nor can He be option two—self-caused—because nothing preexists itself to start itself. Thus God must be the third option—uncaused.

The Bible claims that God is the eternal, uncaused One behind everything else. In Exodus 3:14 He refers to Himself as the great "I AM," pure self-existence. Scripture denies a beginning of God when it calls Him eternal or everlasting. "[T]he LORD is the true God; he is the living God, the *eternal* King" (Jeremiah 10:10, emphasis added). "Before the mountains were born or you brought forth the earth and the world, from everlasting to everlasting you are God" (Psalm 90:2).

God eternally exists, complete and self-sufficient. He didn't create the world to fill a need in Himself. He doesn't depend on the universe or us to fill any lack within Himself. No other deserves worship, praise, and adoration. God did not begin; He will not end; He simply is, and we should praise Him for it. "Stand up and praise the LORD your God, who is from *everlasting to everlasting*" (Nehemiah 9:5, emphasis added).

How Can God Allow Evil?

We wonder how someone can cruise the streets shooting strangers from the trunk of a car. We reel in shock over a tornado that rips apart a neighborhood killing dozens of people. Those events depict two kinds of evil, called by theologians, moral evil and natural evil. Christianity's skeptics point to both as evidence that God cannot be. But the presence of evil confronts all religions and worldviews, not just Christianity.

Evil is not a thing or substance, but the lack of something good. Deafness, for instance, is not a "thing," but the absence of hearing. Natural evil is a disruption in the physical world that hurts humans, such as a flood, an earthquake, or cancer. Moral evil results from moral beings' decisions and actions that violate God's will, such as stealing, racism, or war.

But if God is all-good, all-knowing, and all-loving, how can there be evil? Those factors present a complex riddle leading some to reject God's goodness or knowledge or love, or to deny the reality of evil. Let's address two questions: Where did evil come from? And, can evil

GOD **34**

and the Christian God both be real?

When we hear accounts of evil, our gut reaction is to blame God. He created the world, so we naturally assume that He is somehow the source of the evil within it. But the Bible says that all God made was "very good" (Genesis 1:31). Soon thereafter, however, evil was introduced by Lucifer, who was created good but free, and used his freedom to rebel against his Creator. Then, through the serpent in the Garden, he enticed the first human pair to also rebel against God. The result was the fall of the human race, and evil became part of our world. The point is that God was not the source of evil—Satan was, and now we are.

Theologians through the ages have tried in different ways to resolve the problem of evil. One was mentioned above—creatures with free will, and thus the potential for evil, introduced it into our world. We should also recall that the cosmic game has not ended. God may yet act in a way that explains why He allows evil at all. This world is not the best of all possible worlds, but it may be the best *way* to such a world. An eternity that enjoys victory over evil is apparently better than an eternity that never knew evil.

We may not see it at the time, but God sometimes even converts evil into good. Joseph's brothers sold him into slavery—an unimaginable evil deed. But God used that terrible turn of events to get Joseph into the Prime Minister's seat of Egypt from which he rescued Israel from famine. Joseph later made that exact point: "you meant evil against me; *but* God meant it for good," (Genesis 50:20, NKJV).

In summary, we cannot blame God for evil. It originated by free creatures' choice. God is working toward a better world than the present one, better as a result of allowing evil than if He had not. He even converts evil into good. In the midst of this fallen world, we must trust Him and His promise to work all things for good (Romans 8:28). God is our Victor over evil.

How Could God Send Anyone to Hell?

Today many people joke about hell or consider it a nightmare left over from the Dark Ages. They ask how God could allow such a place. How could He send people there and still be moral? The idea of hell is so gut-wrenching that we almost can't think of it. We might begin by remembering that our *feelings* about God and hell have nothing to do with what is true.

Hell is the place and state of final punishment for the wicked, those forever separated from God and His glory and the hope and joy and life He gives. God did not make hell for humans but for Satan and his angels (Matthew 25:41). Humans go there as the result of rejecting God, expressing their persistent desire to avoid Him. He grants their wish, deporting them to the place of their dreams—absence from Him, the central aspect of hell (2 Thessalonians 1:9).

Having just stood before His judgment, seeing His indescribable glory, then being banished from His

35 GOD

presence, the lost soul's last memory prior to hell is God and everything good. Hell's inhabitant suffers physical and mental anguish, knowing he's forever in that miserable state. He will hopelessly grieve and regret forever what he missed by rejecting God and His merciful plan of escape.

I believe we miss the point when we say, "God sends people to hell." But isn't He involved with their eternal destiny? Of course, but by a life of rejecting God and His salvation, people choose their own separation from Him. In effect, they get what they wanted by refusing God. In fact, wouldn't heaven be hell for those who hate God? What is God to do, force them to choose Him even though they don't want Him? Perhaps it's an act of grace that God allows them a special place where they can hate Him to their heart's content.

But why is hell required at all? The answer lies in the nature of God. Most of what we hear of God today is that He is love. And He is! Far more loving than we imagine or understand. But God is also just, and His justice demands reward and punishment. He will balance the scales of His perfect justice even though it takes eternity to do so. His very nature requires sin to be paid for, or He wouldn't be God.

Amazingly, God provided the payment Himself—His

own Son, Jesus Christ. God poured out His righteous wrath on Christ while He was dying on the cross. What inconceivable love! But hell is available for those who refuse God's payment and wish to pay it themselves. He prefers that they not (2 Peter 3:9), but He allows them to if they want.

God is gracious to everyone for eternity. He supplies exactly what they desire, a place suited for those who want Him—heaven; and a place suited for those who don't—hell. Our not liking the notion of hell doesn't mean we can nullify God's justice or prevent Him from making a perfect place for those who hate Him.

What About Those Who Never Heard?

Missions experts tell us that only half of the world's population have heard of Jesus Christ. And that percentage was higher in the past. The possible implications are terrifying. Could God allow someone to go to hell who never heard His plan of salvation through Christ?

We don't have a full answer because the Bible doesn't address the question as directly as we ask it. The two most common responses are: (1) God saves people who respond positively to general revelation, even if they never hear the gospel. And (2) God will take it upon Himself to get the gospel to those who positively respond to general revelation. The following comments summarize Norm Geisler's treatment of the issue.[3] Let's revisit the two main views.

1. Because God is love He sent His Son to die for everyone (John 3:16; 1 John 2:2). Because He's just He shows no favoritism to anyone (Romans 2:11). Therefore, God would not allow someone to go to hell

GOD 36

who never heard His message of love through Christ. Defenders of this position site Romans 2:6-7 for support: "God 'will give to each person according to what he has done.' To those who by persistence in doing good seek glory, honor and immortality, he will give eternal life." People who haven't heard the gospel form the context of this passage (Romans 2:14). Therefore, proponents of this view conclude that God grants eternal life to those who seek Him based on their receptivity to general revelation alone.

2. The position of the reformers and most evangelicals is that salvation comes only by hearing and accepting the gospel. Acts 4:12 is clear: "Salvation is found in no one else, for there is no other name under heaven given to men by which we must be saved." Apart from the name of Christ, there is no salvation. But a just and loving God will get the gospel to those who react positively to general revelation. Romans 2:6-7, in fact, does not say that those who never hear will be given eternal life. The recipients of eternal life will be those who "seek . . . immortality," apparently referring to their favorable response to general revelation. God can and does send His message throughout the world via TV, radio, printed material, and missionaries. He is also capable of giving direct visions, although this seems less

common than more conventional methods.

God maintains His justice. No undeserving person goes to hell. Since all have sinned (Romans 3:23), all deserve hell. Romans 1:20 also says that all are without excuse as a result of receiving and rejecting God's general revelation. According to Paul, those rejecters have "suppressed the truth" (Romans 1:18). But God also keeps His love intact. He is ready and willing to forgive sin and grant eternal life. He took it upon Himself to provide a way of escaping His judgment. According to Jesus, we are the ones unwilling to turn to Him (Matthew 23:37). Only those who reject God's truth, revealed to them one way or another, go to hell.

Did Anyone See Him?

An eyewitness can make or break a court case. Additional witnesses confirm the story, adding credence to the evidence. The eyewitness testimony about Jesus is vast and compelling. Thousands heard Him teach and saw His miracles; hundreds watched Him die and saw His resurrected body.

Our accounts of Jesus come from eyewitnesses who recorded their own and others' encounters with Him. Two of the gospels, Matthew and John, were written by Jesus' disciples. Mark was not one of the Twelve, but was an eyewitness and largely recorded the stories of Peter, another disciple. Luke did not see Christ, but thoroughly researched the records of those who did (Luke 1:1-4). So all four Gospels are eyewitness reports.

But are those guys credible? Could they have had other motives? Consider the outcome of their commitment to Jesus. As far as we can tell from history, all the original Twelve except John gave their lives for believing that Jesus was who He said He was. And frauds don't die for what they know is a lie. They also wrote many

37 JESUS

embarrassing self-incriminations such as their lack of faith, their slowness to learn, their desire to be the top dog. Such humility is not the trait of deceivers.

Historians generally believe the first three Gospels were written in the fifties and sixties AD, within one generation of Jesus' time. Even skeptics date them no later than the eighties or nineties, the date for John's gospel. Either timeframe is within the life expectancy of witnesses who could have debunked falsehoods in the text. Legends don't work into written records when eyewitnesses are still around to discredit the fiction. Furthermore, if the Gospel writers were frauds, making up or manipulating the facts, would they have recorded so many details capable of being verified or falsified? That seems unlikely.

As we summarize their view of Jesus, let's remember that all the New Testament writers except Luke were monotheistic Jews, believers in one God and that He is one. But they ascribed powers to Jesus that only God possesses: creating the universe (Colossians 1:16), raising the dead (John 11:38-44), forgiving sins (Matthew 9:2; Mark 2:5; Luke 7:48). They linked Jesus' name with the Father's and the Spirit's (Matthew 28:19; 2 Corinthians 13:14). They described Jesus in terms reserved for Deity: "The First and the Last" (Revelation

1:17; 22:13), "That great Shepherd" (Hebrews 13:20), and the judge of the world (John 5:26-27; 2 Timothy 4:1). And they bluntly called Him "God" (John 20:28; Titus 2:13; John 1:1).

Other eyewitnesses include the fanatical Pharisee, Saul of Tarsus. After seeing the resurrected Christ while traveling to Damascus to arrest Christians (Acts 9), he became Christianity's staunchest proponent, known as the apostle Paul. Perhaps more shocking is his record of the resurrected Christ appearing to over five hundred witnesses at once (1 Corinthians 15:6). By specifying that most of them were still alive when he wrote, he was challenging skeptics to go ask them. Paul wouldn't have risked the public humiliation of rebuttal if he wasn't convinced they would back up his account.

Many eyewitnesses saw Jesus, and many saw His resurrected body. Their stories were recorded by multiple, credible authors for the rest of the world to read. He lived, taught, died, and rose again for all to see, and they did (Acts 26:26).

One of a Kind

Almost everyone concedes that Jesus is one of history's great men. Christians declare that He's more than great, He's one of a kind. But is Jesus really unique? What about Moses, Israel's law-giver; or Muhammad, founder of Islam; or the leaders of various Eastern religions; or the famous philosophers of ancient Greece? How do they compare to Jesus? What does He possess that they can't match?

First, Jesus' birth is unique. Centuries before His time, the Old Testament prophet Micah announced where He would be born: "But you, Bethlehem . . . , though you are small among the clans of Judah, out of you will come for me one who will be ruler over Israel, whose origins are from of old, from ancient times" (Micah 5:2). Isaiah prophesied that Christ would be conceived and born of a virgin: "Therefore the Lord himself will give you a sign: The virgin will be with child and will give birth to a son, and will call him Immanuel" (Isaiah 7:14).

Furthermore, unlike any others, Jesus lived a perfect life, "tempted in every way, just as we are—yet was without sin" (Hebrews 4:15). He performed many miracles, even raising the dead. Consider John's account: "Jesus called in a loud voice, 'Lazarus, come out!' The dead man came out, his hands and feet wrapped with strips of linen, and a cloth around his face" (John 11:43-44). Jesus even claimed to be God. When asked if He was the Son of God, He replied, "You are right in saying I am" (Luke 22:70).

But all that is surpassed by His pre-proclaimed resurrection, appearance to over five hundred people at once, and ascension to heaven. Matthew records Jesus' prediction in 17:9: "Don't tell anyone what you have seen, until the Son of Man has been raised from the dead." Paul asserts that Jesus then "appeared to more than five hundred of the brothers at the same time, most of whom [were] still living" (1 Corinthians 15:6). Later, in plain view, Jesus was "taken up before their very eyes, and a cloud hid him from their sight" (Acts 1:9).

No résumé compares to that. Moses, the greatest Old Testament prophet, never claimed deity, and his law couldn't do what Jesus did—save people from their sins. Mohammad went to war to force converts to Islam. He did no miracles and never alleged that he was divine. The gurus and leaders of Hinduism, Buddhism, and Taoism don't do miracles, and the few who assert divine status can't back it up. Socrates, Plato, and Aristotle were great thinkers, but they didn't answer ultimate questions about life after death or declare that their ideas came from God.

No other leader claimed to be God's Son and then provided evidence by living a sinless life and performing astounding miracles like raising the dead. The most important distinction between Jesus and all others is His resurrection. Every other world leader died and remained dead. Jesus died but came back to life. He is truly unique.

Who Does He Think He Is — God?

Jesus' critics say He was a great, moral teacher but He never claimed to be God. They argue that His followers created the legend of His deity after He was gone. That charge raises several questions: What did Jesus say about Himself? What difference does it make if He said He was God? What alternatives remain about His identity if He was not God?

A person who declares himself God reduces the options as to what he truly is. If he's not God only two alternatives are possible. First, he could be nuts, a lunatic. Many people in mental hospitals and a few on the street claim deity, but their lives and character soon reveal otherwise. Jesus' life and character, however, support His claim. Second, he could be a deceiver, a deliberate liar. Religious charlatans are common, but they're eventually exposed as frauds. Jesus' miracles, good deeds, and sacrificial life argue that He was genuine. But did He say He was God? The Gospels record

39 JESUS

three kinds of evidence that reveal Jesus' belief in His own deity.

First, He directly said so. Consider John 8:58: "Before Abraham was born, I am!" This alleges more than prior existence—"I am" was the special name God gave to identify Himself when talking to Moses in Exodus 3:14. Those who heard Jesus use it thought He was claiming deity because they took up rocks to stone Him—the punishment for blasphemy. He also admitted His deity in Luke 22:70 during His trial for His life: "They all asked, 'Are you then the Son of God?' He replied, 'You are right in saying I am.'"

Second, He said and did several things to equate Himself with God. For instance, in John 5:17-18 He presumed a special relationship, "He was even calling God his own Father, making himself equal with God." He also modified God's law: "You have heard that it was said . . . But I tell you . . . ." (Matthew 5:21-22); and, "Heaven and earth will pass away, but my words will never pass away" (Matthew 24:35). Furthermore, He declared Himself the only way to God in John 14:6: "I am the way and the truth and the life. No one comes to the Father except through me." He even forgave sins: "Then Jesus said to her, 'Your sins are forgiven'" (Luke 7:48); and He claimed to be the final judge in eternity: "The Father . . .

has entrusted all judgment to the Son" (John 5:22).

Third, He accepted others' statements of His deity including their worship, "When they saw him, they worshiped him" (Matthew 28:17); their prayer, "You may ask me for anything in my name, and I will do it" (John 14:14); and their direct admission of His deity, "Then those who were in the boat worshiped him, saying, 'Truly you are the Son of God'" (Matthew 14:33).

Jesus saw Himself as deity, the One through whom God entered the human race and through whom God spoke and acted. Could He be wrong? That's highly unlikely given the evidence of His miracles and resurrection. We can be sure of one thing—He did see Himself as God, and if He was not, He was no great, moral teacher. He left us only three options: He was either a raving lunatic, a devious liar, or the Lord of the universe. Whoever we believe He is sets the path of our life and our eternity.

Is He Who He Said He Was?

Christianity stands on the belief that Jesus Christ is God. But is that true? What evidence supports His claim and His disciples' belief that He was deity? Let's consider three categories of evidence: (1) He fulfilled Old Testament prophecy. (2) He lived a sinless life. (3) He rose from the dead.

First, note that Jesus fulfilled almost two hundred detailed prophecies written centuries before His time. Critics allege that Jesus deliberately orchestrated His life to fraudulently fulfill these. Now think about that. Could He have arranged His family line through Abraham (Genesis 22:18; Matthew 1:1), the tribe of Judah (Genesis 49:10; Luke 3:33), and the royal house of David (2 Samuel 7:12-13; Matthew 1:1)? How could He plan to be born in Bethlehem (Micah 5:2; Luke 2:4-7)? Were His many spectacular miracles part of His counterfeit life (Isaiah 35:5-6; Matthew 9:35)? And did He orchestrate His own crucifixion by manipulating the Jewish religious leaders and the Roman government to conspire against Him? And fulfilling that crucifix-

JESUS **40**

ion included numerous details anticipated by the Old Testament (Psalm 22; Matthew 27:31; Luke 23:33; John 19:23-24). And most of all, how did He falsely fulfill the prophecy that He would rise from the dead (Psalm 16:10; Mark 16:6)? Add to all this Jesus' stunning revelation after He rose from the dead that the entire Old Testament pointed to Him (Luke 24:25-27).

Second, Jesus displayed divine traits such as knowing people's thoughts and future actions (Matthew 26:31-35; Luke 9:46-47; 11:17), controlling the forces of nature (Matthew 8:26-27; Mark 6:38-45), and healing paralysis and disease (Matthew 8:2-3; 9:6-7; 9:27-30). He achieved something else that no one has done—a sinless life. Even in the presence of His opponents, who were determined to bring Him down, He challenged anyone to find Him guilty of sin, and none could (John 8:46). Sinlessness itself does not prove deity. But claiming deity, then living perfectly, backs up the claim quite nicely. Perhaps most convincing of His sinlessness, His friends, those who knew Him best, said the same (1 Peter 1:19; 2:22; 2 Corinthians 5:21).

Third, Jesus' resurrection, His greatest and most well-documented miracle, is unduplicated in any other religion. And this unprecedented miracle wasn't the product of wishful thinking or mere speculation. On the contrary, according to Luke, Jesus "gave many convincing proofs that he was alive" (Acts 1:3). Paul said He appeared to over five hundred people at one time after His resurrection (1 Corinthians 15:6). This ability to return from death reflects the divine trait of immortality, and His prediction of His resurrection reveals His divine foreknowledge. Above all else, the Resurrection confirms Him and His claim to deity.

Jesus said He was God and provided evidence by fulfilling Old Testament prophecy, living a sinless life, and returning from the dead. That evidence should lead us to Paul's conclusion that all the fullness of God dwells in Him (Colossians 1:19), and He's worthy of our worship. The next two chapters will focus in more detail on His miracles and fulfillment of Old Testament prophecy.

What a Show!

Miracles are supernatural events, transcending or suspending natural laws. God's purpose in them is to glorify Himself, or confirm His message through a spokesman, or provide reason to believe in Himself. Miracle stories are scattered throughout the Bible, many about Jesus. They point to Jesus' power over death, demons, and disease; confirm His divine status; and, according to Isaiah, reveal the Messiah's presence (Isaiah 35:5-6).

The list of Jesus' miracles is long and diverse. He walked on water (Matthew 14:25), multiplied fish and bread (John 6:11), healed invalids (John 5:5-15), restored sight to the blind (John 9:1-7), cured lepers (Matthew 8:1-3), expelled demons (Mark 1:34), calmed the storm (Mark 4:37-39), and raised the dead (John 11:38-44). It doesn't get more impressive than that.

His miracles were not added to the Bible generations later to embellish Jesus' life story. They were embedded in the accounts early in the recording of what He did and said. Even critical scholars who are not sympathetic to an early dating of the Gospels almost universally

41 JESUS

recognize the stories of Jesus' miracles as authentic. They admit that miracles were already included in the sources the Gospel writers used in their preparation to write their own accounts. Ancient nonChristian sources also acknowledge Jesus' miracles.

Jesus understood His miracles differently from the way other miracle workers saw theirs. He used them to link Himself to the kingdom of God (Luke 11:20). He interpreted them as God's invasion of the natural order through Himself. The combination of Jesus' supernatural feats and His claim to be God are unique. One without the other leaves room for doubt, but the two together are shocking and demand serious reflection.

His Jewish audience recognized His miracles for what they were and admitted that Jesus could be the Messiah. After healing a man possessed by a demon, "All the people were astonished and said, 'Could this be the Son of David?'" (Matthew 12:23). Even the Pharisees, who opposed Jesus vehemently, recognized the reality of the miracle. They saw it for themselves. So they couldn't deny it happened. But rather than acknowledge God's presence in Jesus, they ascribed His power to the Devil (Matthew 12:24).

One of their top teachers, however, privately stated the inescapable conclusion, "He came to Jesus at night and said, 'Rabbi, we know you are a teacher who has come from God. For no one could perform the miraculous signs you are doing if God were not with him'" (John 3:2). Those who saw His miracles should have wondered about the same thing the disciples asked after seeing Jesus still the storm: "Who is this? Even the wind and the waves obey him!" (Mark 4:41). They could have drawn the same conclusion Peter did, "You are the Christ, the Son of the living God" (Matthew 16:16). Jesus' extraordinary miracles reveal that He was more than a mere prophet—He was God's one and only Son. In effect, by His miracles, He was announcing, "I am the One foretold by the prophets—God in human flesh. If you want proof, look at My miracles."

They Called It; He Did It

Ancient Jews could have recognized the Messiah because their Scriptures prophesy about Him. Peter noted as much when referring to Jesus' crucifixion and resurrection: "This is how God fulfilled what he had foretold through all the prophets, saying that his Christ [the Messiah] would suffer" (Acts 3:18). Paul also relied on Scripture to present Jesus as Messiah: "[He] went into the synagogue, and . . . reasoned with them from the Scriptures, explaining and proving that the Christ had to suffer and rise from the dead. 'This Jesus I am proclaiming to you is the Christ,' he said" (Acts 17:2-3).

Critics raise several challenges against the Christian belief that Jesus fulfilled Old Testament prophecy.

1. Weren't the prophecies written after Jesus' time? In other words, were the authors writing history instead of prophecy? No. Even the most skeptical biblical critics date the latest Old Testament writings hundreds of years before Jesus' time. And these prophecies were too precise to have been "fulfilled" in the vague way that modern psychics claim fulfillment of their predictions.

2. Don't Christians misinterpret Old Testament passages to make them point to Christ when those texts don't do that? The New Testament sometimes does *apply* parts of the Old Testament to Christ which were not written directly about Him. But that misses the point—many Old Testament prophecies point unmistakably to Christ. For the skeptic to use this argument, she must show that *no* Old Testament prophecies were predictive of Christ and fulfilled in Him.

3. Perhaps Jesus manipulated His own circumstances to "fulfill" prophecies to look like He was the Messiah. But Jesus could not have controlled most of those events, especially His lineage, birthplace, miracles, crucifixion, and resurrection. Nor was it consistent with His well-documented integrity to play the role of a fraud.

4. Maybe Jesus fulfilled those prophecies by accident—He just happened to be in the right place at the right time. Mathematicians have crunched the numbers to figure out that possibility. The odds of Jesus fulfilling even eight Messianic prophecies by chance are one in a number with seventeen zeroes after it. Accidentally accomplishing that would be a miracle itself. By way of comparison, studies on psychics' predictions reveal a less than 10 percent accuracy rate.

5. Some suggest that the prophets made false predictions as well as true, but the Old Testament records only the true ones. Two problems arise with this view. (1) The theory is pure speculation—no evidence exists that the inspired Old Testament prophets made wrong prophecies. (2) Even if it were true, it still doesn't account for all the prophecies that came true. The Bible's ability to predict the future and Christ's fulfillment of it still stand.

6. Not all of the Bible's predictions have come about. True. But some were conditional like Jonah's prophecy of God wiping out Nineveh. So when the people repented, God withheld His predicted judgment. Others could not have been fulfilled yet because they're tied to Christ's second coming.

Efforts to dismiss Jesus' fulfillment of Old Testament prophecy can't escape the obvious—He did! Their fulfillment is a miracle that points to His identity—God's Messiah.

Others Knew

Do ancient sources outside the New Testament speak about Christ? Is He even mentioned elsewhere? Uninformed critics may think not. A few even assert that Jesus never existed. But many ancient records, Christian and nonChristian, confirm the New Testament accounts about Christ. Ancient historians, government officials, nonChristian religious writers, and others leave an irrefutable record of the reality of Jesus.[4]

Historians: Jewish writer Josephus twice refers to Christ in his first-century writings, identifying James as His brother, and referring to Christ's life, crucifixion, claim to be the Messiah, and effect on others. In AD 115 Roman author Tacitus recorded that Christ was crucified by Pontius Pilate, after which a "superstition" (probably the Resurrection) broke out and spread from Judea to Rome. Also early in the second century, Emperor Hadrian's secretary, Suetonius, wrote of Jews who disturbed the peace in the previous century over a certain "Chrestus" (Christ). None of those men were sympathetic toward Christianity. Thus, their reports cannot be

43

JESUS

accused of bias in favor of Christ.

Government Officials: About AD 111, Pliny the Younger, Roman Governor of Bithynia, reported his arrest of Christians to Emperor Trajan. He described them as committed followers of Christ to whom they sang hymns "as to a god." Trajan wrote back with guidelines for dealing with them. According to Christian historian Eusebius (ca. 265-339), Emperor Hadrian (reign, 117-138) wrote a similar letter to an official in Asia. It's hard to imagine Roman Emperors giving directions about how to control followers of someone who never existed.

Gnostic Writings: Consider the following second-century books: *The Gospel of Truth* substantiates the reality of Jesus by referring to His incarnation, teaching, crucifixion, and resurrection. *The Apocryphon of John* contains a conversation with references to Jesus. Even if the conversation never occurred, the story reveals the awareness that Jesus lived, and when the Gospels say He did. *The Gospel of Thomas* mentions Jesus' death, as well as titles for Him such as "The Son of Man," "The Resurrected One," and "The All of the Universe." *The Treatise on Resurrection* speaks of the deity of Jesus, who became man, died, and rose again.

Others: The Jewish writings known as the Talmud say that Jesus was crucified on Passover eve for sorcery (miracles) and heresy. In his second-century critique of Christianity, Greek author Lucian of Samosata reveals that Christians worshiped Jesus who was crucified for introducing new doctrines. Mara Bar-Serapion was a Syrian who lived between the late first and early third centuries. In a letter to his son, he compared a wise Jewish "King" to Socrates and Pythagoras. Based on his description, scholars believe he's referring to Jesus. Even the Koran refers to Jesus and His miracles, His mother Mary and His disciples, and His death and ascension.

No other religious founder is as well documented as Jesus. NonChristian records of His existence far surpass the historical support for Zoroaster, Buddha, Mohammed, and others. Even without the New Testament, we could construct a rough outline of His life. Those who reject Jesus as nonhistorical reveal their ignorance of history or bias against what it says.

JESUS' DEATH

Did Jesus Really Die?

In the TV show *CSI*, forensic pathology and medical research uncover the circumstances of death. These modern sciences can also tell us about Jesus' death. Some skeptics claim that Jesus' crucifixion didn't kill Him, and if He didn't die, He didn't rise from the dead. What does medical science say about crucifixion? Could Jesus have survived it?

Before He was crucified He was brutally beaten with a whip designed to inflict maximum damage. It was made of leather thongs with pieces of bone and lead on the ends to rip the skin, exposing the muscles and organs. Soldiers assigned to this duty sometimes continued until the backside was laid bare from shoulders to thighs. Some victims died from it. Survivors went into deep shock from massive blood loss.

The victim's arms were then stretched over the crossbeam for six-inch spikes to be driven through the wrists into the wood. When the crossbar was attached to the vertical stake, the feet were nailed to it. The weight of the body pulling against the spikes stretched the arms, dislocated the shoulders, and prevented breathing. The victim had to pull up with his nailed hands and push up on nailed feet to relax the lungs enough to breathe. The victim eventually grew too exhausted to continue and died of asphyxiation.

The release of "blood and water" as described by eyewitnesses (John 19:34) is exactly what medical science expects when a person dies under these conditions. Severe shock accelerated the heart rate leading to heart failure, depositing fluid in the membrane around the heart and lungs. So Jesus was probably already dead when the soldier speared Him in the side, piercing His rib cage, lung, and heart. If He was still alive, the spear thrust would have killed Him.

Sometimes the Romans wanted to accelerate death, so they smashed the legs with a steel bar, ending the victim's efforts to breath. Asphyxiation quickly followed. But Jesus had died by the time the soldiers came with the steal bar, so they didn't need to break His legs (John 19:33). These were professional executioners who knew when a person was dead or only looked dead. They were highly motivated not to make mistakes because if the condemned person avoided death, they would pay with their own lives. And Pilate double-checked with the execution squad to make sure Jesus was dead (Mark

15:44-45).

Even if they had erred, Jesus would have to survive an impossible ordeal to fake a resurrection: survive three days in a tomb without medical care (Matthew 27:60); survive despite being unable to breathe from the mummy-like burial wrappings that also prevented Him from unwrapping Himself (John 19:39-40); remove the huge stone; fight off the soldiers guarding the tomb; walk away on wounded feet; and then convince over five hundred people that He had come back from the dead and they should worship Him as God. Believing that scenario requires more faith than believing in His death and resurrection.

Why Is Jesus' Tomb Empty?

Skeptics deny the resurrection of Christ, and to support their rejection, they propose alternate theories to explain the empty tomb. Their best three efforts are known as the swoon theory, the theft theory, and the wrong tomb theory. Let's briefly consider each. Does any one of them present a viable alternative to Jesus' resurrection recorded in the Bible?

The first proposes that Jesus didn't die—He only passed out or appeared to die. When He was laid on the cold slab in the tomb, He revived, got up, and left. But this seems physically impossible. When Christ was nailed to the cross, He had already suffered severe tortures that killed some victims before they could be crucified. And crucifixion was a proven method of execution, performed by a special squad of Roman soldiers, experts in their craft. They were convinced, as was everyone else, that Jesus was dead. Even if He had survived the tortures, the crucifixion, and the spear thrust into His side, this theory struggles. How could Jesus wiggle out of the tightly wound grave clothes, remove the massive stone to exit the tomb, fight off or evade the guards, walk away on nail-pierced feet, and then convince hundreds of people that He had been resurrected? This theory is so unlikely that most contemporary skeptics reject it as simply preposterous.

The theft theory claims that Jesus' disciples stole the body. According to Matthew 28:11-15, this explanation was created by the Jewish leadership. But the disciples would be incapable of overpowering the armed guards posted at the tomb. Nor would the guards have fallen asleep, because that offense was punishable by death. And would anyone be able to sleep through the noise made by several men breaking into a sealed tomb by removing a large, secured stone and carrying away the body from inside? Would the disciples have been motivated to even consider such a theft knowing their leader, who had promised them so much, had now been publicly executed as a criminal? Would the disciples willingly go to their deaths in the following years for their belief in the Resurrection if they knew it was a hoax? This theory fails serious scrutiny, and today's scholars have abandoned it also.

The wrong tomb theory originated in the early twentieth century. It claims that in the dark, early that Sunday morning, the women followers of Jesus, and then everyone else, simply went to the wrong tomb, an empty one. Jesus' tomb, with His body inside, was elsewhere. This theory starts poorly, being based on a careless reading of the biblical text. The burial site was known by the women and by others. Even if they had made such an error, they would notice their mistake when morning light came and then simply go to the right tomb. Most important, the Jewish leaders or the Romans could have ended the whole resurrection uproar by just going to the right tomb and producing the body. This theory had so many deficiencies from the start that it never rallied much support.

More problems exist for the proposed theories than are presented in these brief summaries. But they introduce the challenge faced by alternate understandings of what the Bible records—that Jesus died, was buried, and came back to life. No reasonable alternate theory exists. Our faith is not based on wild-eyed fantasies, but on the only rational understanding of the historical record—Jesus died and came back to life.

He Just Keeps Showing Up

To verify Jesus' resurrection, evidence must demonstrate that He was seen alive after His death. In Acts 1:3 Luke tells us just that—the disciples repeatedly saw Jesus over a forty-day period after His executioners pronounced Him dead and sealed His body in a tomb.

Of the twelve recorded appearances, the most stunning is Paul's claim that Jesus appeared to over five hundred eyewitnesses at one time (1 Corinthians 15:3-7). Scholars say this statement is embedded within a creed dated less than a decade after Christ's death. That early date provides great historical reliability because too little time had passed to stretch the facts. And Paul provocatively declared that most of those eye-witnesses were still alive at the time he wrote. He was apparently challenging his readers to question the witnesses to confirm his story.

Christ's post-death appearances cannot be dismissed as nonevents. So skeptics devise other explanations to try to refute them. One option is that the witnesses lied or started a legend. But legends develop over time, and the records of Jesus' appearances occurred too soon after the event for such legendary enhancement. Hinting that the disciples lied is extremely far-fetched because they were tortured and martyred for this belief. Someone might die for what he believes is true, but no one dies for what he knows is false. This suggestion just won't fly.

Some propose that Jesus' followers suffered hallucinations or were highly suggestible. This view says the witnesses just saw what they wanted to believe. But ancient Jews believed the righteous dead went to heaven to await a general resurrection at the end of time. Their hallucinations would not have imagined Jesus returning to them in resurrected form because that belief was not in their theological framework. Furthermore, hallucinations are rare events that occur only to individuals, not to groups. They happen to people who expect them, but the disciples were not expecting Jesus to appear. They had lost hope and returned to their fishing business. This theory also does not explain how the disciples physically touched Jesus nor how He ate with them. And if Jesus' appearances were merely hallucinations, why didn't someone just produce the body and end the rumor?

The biblical documents claim that after His death, Jesus appeared several times to many people in different groups and situations for several weeks. Names of the witnesses and details of the encounters are listed. The accounts of physical contact with Jesus even include His crucifixion scars. The resurrection narrative is not a poorly documented fantasy, only verifiable by one or two people who could have twisted the facts. The evidence is overwhelming that Jesus was seen alive by hundreds of people after He died. His resurrection was real, it changed their lives, and it changes lives today.

More Resurrection Evidence

Jesus' death, empty grave, and later appearances introduce a compelling case for the Resurrection. But is there more evidence? Did it make a real difference or did early Christians create and grow a legend? What can we learn about the alleged Resurrection by observing its effect on the people and society of the time?

Some who believed in Jesus after His death were skeptics during His life. Take Jesus' half-brother James. He didn't buy Jesus' claim to deity; in fact, James thought his older brother was nuts (Mark 3:21). But after the Resurrection, he became the leader of the Jerusalem church and was stoned to death for his belief that Jesus was God. Something extraordinary had happened. Paul tells us that James saw Jesus alive after He died (1 Corinthians 15:7). Consider Paul (Saul) himself, who hated Christians and everything they stood for. He saw them as a threat to his Judaism, so he did all he could to have them arrested and executed (Acts 9:1-2). Then, out of the blue, he converted to Christianity. Why? What happened? An encounter with the risen Christ turned his life around (Acts 9:3-5).

Something also transformed Jesus' disciples. Their first reaction to His arrest and crucifixion was to scatter, cowardly hiding from the authorities, fearing the same fate as their leader (John 20:19). He was dead and so were their dreams. But something soon compelled them to publicly preach Christ as God, returned from the dead—a shocking heresy among Jews who believed no one would be resurrected until the end of the world. The disciples faced arrest, torture, and execution for believing in Jesus, but not one recanted. Some people are willing to endure torture and death for a lie if they believe it's true. But no one willingly accepts pain and suffering and death for what they know is a lie, and the disciples were in a position to know if the Resurrection was false. They knew it was true, and it changed them forever.

Why were Jesus' enemies unable to produce His body? Jewish and Roman authorities knew where the tomb was. They could have ended the resurrection rumors by simply displaying the body. The new movement would have died instantly (1 Corinthians 15:14,17). But in their confusion, all they could come up with was a scheme to bribe the guards at the tomb to say the disciples stole the body (Matthew 28:12-15), a far-fetched theory we considered in chapter 45.

How do we explain the origin of the church? Only the Resurrection could make Christianity distinct from Judaism. Without it, what was the point for Jews sticking with the new movement? They weren't disgruntled with their Jewish heritage, which they believed had come from God. But they reinterpreted the Mosaic Law, stopped offering sacrifices, worshiped on Sunday instead of the Sabbath, and preached Jesus as God. They memorialized His death in communion, and initiated new members with baptism, another ceremony that celebrated His death and resurrection.

Despite severe persecution, this new movement spread so fast and far that within a few years it covered the Roman Empire including Caesar's household (Philippians 1:13; 4:22). Even their enemies said they turned the world upside down (Acts 17:6, NKJV). What could account for this irresistible, Empire-conquering growth if Jesus were still dead?

BODILY RESURRECTION

Was It Really Him?

What is the nature of Jesus' resurrection body? Some who believe Jesus rose from the grave don't believe in His *bodily* resurrection. According to them, the body that rose from the grave was not the same body that was crucified and buried, only a spiritual body. But Jews of the time believed in the oneness of the person—the unity of body and spirit. The idea of resurrecting one part of the person (the spirit) and not the other part (the body) didn't occur to them. A nonphysical resurrection would make no sense to them. And the New Testament records strong evidence that Jesus' post-resurrection body was physical.

According to the New Testament Gospels (Mark 9:9; Luke 24:26), history (Acts 3:15), and Epistles (Romans 4:24), Jesus was resurrected "from the dead." The word translated "from" is *ek*, which means "out from among." Among what?—the dead bodies, the corpses. The implication is that Jesus' corpse, His physical body, not just a spiritual body, was resurrected. Consistent with that understanding, the New Testament word for "body" (*soma*) is used only for a physical body.

The empty tomb is perhaps the most obvious evidence for Jesus' bodily resurrection. When the angels explained Jesus' absence from the tomb, they implied a bodily resurrection: "He is not here; he has risen, just as he said. Come and see the place where he lay" (Matthew 28:6). What was laid in that place was His corpse, His physical body, and that's what the angels said was gone. The physical body was missing because it was resurrected.

The disciples were understandably shocked when Jesus showed up after being killed before their eyes. In response to their amazement, Jesus said in Luke 24:39 that His body was physical, "Look at my hands and my feet. It is I myself! Touch me and see; a ghost does not have flesh and bones, as you see I have." He even told Thomas, who didn't believe anything easily, to feel His wounds: "Put your finger here; see my hands. Reach out your hand and put it into my side" (John 20:27). "They [even] gave him a piece of broiled fish, and he took it and ate it in their presence" (Luke 24:42-43). What else could He do to prove that His resurrected body was physical rather than just a spirit?

If someone rejects the bodily resurrection, how does she explain the plainly physical nature of Christ's post-resurrection appearances? Were they hallucinations? That suggestion fails for two reasons: (1) Hallucinations don't appear to multiple people in many places over a period of time as Jesus did. And (2) that proposal doesn't account for the empty tomb. Hallucinations would not remove the body from its grave, but it was gone.

In summary, the basic question still stands: If the Resurrection were only spiritual, what happened to the physical body? It was never found. Furthermore, all the Gospel accounts of the Resurrection refer to it as physical. Not one even hints of a nonphysical appearance. Nothing explains the evidence other than a bodily resurrection.

A Prophesied Resurrection

The Old Testament pictured Israel's return from exile as resurrection. For instance, Hosea 13:14 states, "I will ransom them from the power of the grave; I will redeem them from death." But the second half of that verse asks: "Where, O death, are your plagues? Where, O grave, is your destruction?" That sounds familiar because in 1 Corinthians 15:55 Paul applied it to individual resurrection: "Where, O death, is your victory? Where, O death, is your sting?" So Paul believed the Old Testament spoke of individual resurrection.

The psalmist agreed, "God will redeem my life from the grave" (Psalm 49:15). Isaiah says the same: "[Y]our dead will live; their bodies will rise. You who dwell in the dust, wake up and shout for joy. Your dew is like the dew of the morning; the earth will give birth to her dead" (Isaiah 26:19). Daniel 12:2 even distinguishes between the just and the wicked at the resurrection: "Multitudes who sleep in the dust of the earth will awake: some to everlasting life, others to shame and everlasting contempt."

But does the Old Testament prophesy the Messiah's resurrection? The logic of two passages in Isaiah answers, "Yes." First, Isaiah 53:8-9 teaches that the Messiah would die: "For he was cut off from the land of the living; for the transgression of my people he was stricken. He was assigned a grave with the wicked, and with the rich in his death." But according to Isaiah 9:7, He will also reign forever from Jerusalem: "Of the increase of his government and peace there will be no end. He will reign on David's throne and over his kingdom, establishing and upholding it with justice and righteousness from that time on and forever." The only way for the Messiah to die but reign forever is to return from the dead.

David writes in Psalm 16:10, "You will not abandon me to the grave, nor will you let your Holy One see decay." But according to Peter's sermon at Pentecost, David was not speaking about himself but Jesus, whom Peter is presenting as the Messiah. After quoting Psalm 16:10, he explained it to the crowd in the following way: "Brothers, I can tell you confidently that the patriarch David died and was buried, and his tomb is here to this day. But he was a prophet and knew that God had promised him on oath that he would place one of his descendants on his throne. Seeing what was ahead, he spoke of the resurrection of the Christ, that he was not abandoned to the grave, nor did his body see decay. God has raised this Jesus to life, and we are all witnesses of the fact" (Acts 2:29-32).

So the Old Testament did prophesy that the Messiah would return from the dead, as Jesus Himself promised, "The Son of Man is going to be betrayed into the hands of men. They will kill him, and on the third day he will be raised to life" (Matthew 17:22-23).

RESURRECTION AND JESUS' PROPHECY

He Called It

Is it more amazing to return from the dead, or to announce in advance that you will? The only thing that can top either is to do both, and Jesus did. He prepared His followers for His death by telling them ahead of time that He would be killed, but not to worry, He would rise from the grave. "'We are going up to Jerusalem,' he said, 'and the Son of Man will be betrayed to the chief priests and teachers of the law. They will condemn him to death and will hand him over to the Gentiles, who will mock him and spit on him, flog him and kill him. Three days later he will rise'" (Mark 10:33-34). Imagine their shock upon hearing that.

And Jesus didn't offer those predictions when His arrest was imminent and He might make an educated guess, at least about His treatment by the authorities. He announced it early in His ministry, before anyone could possibly foresee coming events. During His first temple cleansing He said, "'Destroy this temple, and I will raise it again in three days.'. . . But the temple he had spoken of was his body" (John 2:19,21). John and the others may not have understood at the time, but they did when it happened.

Jesus' prophecy of His resurrection was not a one-time, off-the-cuff comment that might have been dismissed as a flippant remark. After Peter acknowledged that Jesus was the Messiah, "He then began to teach them that the Son of Man must suffer many things and be rejected by the elders, chief priests and teachers of the law, and that he must be killed and after three days rise again" (Mark 8:31). Note that Jesus *began* teaching them about His resurrection. This doesn't mean He never mentioned it before, as we've already seen, but that He began to emphasize it consistently from that day forward.

We may miss another detail in Jesus' resurrection prediction—He said He would raise Himself. In other words, He announced more than His return from the dead; He said he would come back to life by His *own* power. "No one takes [my life] from me, but I lay it down of my own accord. I have authority to lay it down and authority to take it up again" (John 10:18). That's nothing short of a claim to be the author of life.

It takes courage and confidence to make a bold prediction. Jesus showed both when He announced that He would rise from the grave. Predicting His resurrection, and then pulling it off, is the prime proof of His deity. Nothing could top that for confirming He really was who He said He was. And the implication can't be avoided: If Jesus is deity, He has a claim on my life. But some people willfully reject the evidence. Jesus even predicted that: "He said . . . , 'If they do not listen to Moses and the Prophets, they will not be convinced even if someone rises from the dead'" (Luke 16:31). He always stays one step ahead of His critics.

So What?

The world's religions compete for attention and devotion. Most of them are a collection of ideas—philosophy applied to spiritual topics. Only a few are based on a person: Judaism on Abraham, Buddhism on Gautama, Islam on Mohammed, and Christianity on Christ. Of those four person-centered religions, only Christianity claims that its founder rose from the dead. No records of the other three even hint of an empty tomb for the man behind their faith. But so what if Christ rose from the dead? Does it really make any difference? Let's consider four consequences of His resurrection.

First, the Resurrection verifies the claims of Christ, especially about His identity. His conquest of death demonstrates that He is who He said He was and He did what He said He would. He is deity who died for the sins of the world. If He had remained dead after dying, we would know He was a fraud. But since He negotiated the passage from life to death and back again, how can we explain Him other than to admit that He is deity? Only God holds the keys to life and death, and Jesus obviously held them in His hands.

Second, Christ's resurrection makes Christianity unique. As noted above, no other religion can offer its followers this ultimate conquest—victory over death and the resulting eternal life. The Resurrection is so central to Christianity that Paul says without it Christianity is false. "And if Christ has not been raised, our preaching is useless and so is your faith. . . . You are still in your sins" (1 Corinthians 15:14,17). Christians have always held out the challenge to others—the risk for themselves—to disprove the Resurrection, and they would abandon the faith. Critics have tried for 2,000 years, and none have succeeded yet.

Third, the Resurrection affects our eternity in several ways. Since Jesus overcame death, it no longer threatens Him (Romans 6:9). He thus possesses never-ending life, which He can give to us. In fact, Peter says our new birth and eternal hope are based on the Resurrection (1 Peter 1:3). That's possible, Paul explains, because we're now justified before God as a result of the Resurrection (Romans 4:25). That extraordinary feat displayed God's acceptance of Christ's death for our sins, thus God declares us righteous in Christ. His resurrection also is the basis of our own future resurrection (1 Corinthians 6:14; 2 Corinthians 4:14).

Fourth, the Resurrection impacts our life now. Its power liberates us from sin's control (Romans 6:9-14), and forms the basis for ministry (Acts 1:21-25). It endorses Jesus' teaching and moral example. If we really have found someone who died and returned, doesn't it make sense to listen to His ideas and imitate His life? So the Resurrection gives us a purpose for living. What could be more important than telling others how to cheat death and live forever?

Christianity's gospel wouldn't be good news if Christ were still dead. After all, if He is dead, why bother? But because He's alive again, it's the best news possible. Who wouldn't want to be on the side of a guy who conquered death?

REINCARNATION

Here We Go Again

Persistence pays. If you keep at it, you'll eventually get it right. Does that apply to living repeated lives? Many think so. Most Hindus, Buddhists, Taoists, Sikhs, and Jains believe in reincarnation—the rebirth of the soul into a new body after the previous body dies. In fact, the soul returns many times in different bodies—renewed chances to get it right. With the spread of Eastern religions into the West, almost one fourth of Americans now believe the same.

Most forms of reincarnation are based on karma, the moral law of cause and effect. Our soul carries our karma—our deeds and their consequences—from one life to another. Good deeds elevate one's position in the next life; bad deeds lower it. A very evil person might be reborn as a goat or a snail. We each go through this cycle of life and death thousands of times. Our goal is to accumulate enough good deeds to pay off our karmic debt and escape the cycle of rebirth. In the most common form of reincarnation, if we escape, our personal identity is merged into the One.

Defenders of reincarnation usually present the following arguments: (1) The soul is immortal, so it cannot die or end. Therefore, when a body dies, that soul moves into a new body. (2) The law of karma is the best way to achieve justice. If you don't get what you deserve in this life, you will in the next. (3) Some people recall "past lives" during altered states of consciousness such as hypnosis. Those lives and their memories are believed to be real.

But supporters of reincarnation cannot adequately support their case. First, the soul may be immortal, but that doesn't imply that it returns in a different body. A soul could live in a disembodied state, or in a resurrected body designed to live forever. Also, reincarnation doesn't address issues of justice and evil. It merely attempts to balance the scales, one life at a time, forever. How did the bad karma originate in the first place? Nor does the concept of karma offer a basis for right and wrong—guidance about what to do or not do. So we can't even evaluate deeds as good or bad. Finally, memories of "past lives" don't prove reincarnation. They offer nothing to verify that they are what they claim to be.

The practical consequence of believing in reincarnation and karma is increased suffering. We shouldn't help the poor or crippled or homeless because they're living out the result of their karma from a previous life. You might even add to your own karmic debt by helping them avoid theirs. The lack of improvement in societies that believe in reincarnation also argues against it. If we've each had thousands of lives to improve, why isn't society getting better?

The Bible clearly teaches against reincarnation. It first says we're created, not reincarnated (Genesis 1:27). Jesus taught that we don't pay for prebirth sins (John 9:3). We die once and then face judgment (Hebrews 9:27). God's plan for mankind is based on forgiveness by grace, not perfection by work (Ephesians 2:8). And we have access to the insights of one person, the only one, who died, was buried, and returned from the dead—Jesus—and He said resurrection, not reincarnation, is true.

How Do Scientists Think?

People from the past affect us today, including how we think. English scientist Francis Bacon (1561-1626) believed that we should learn God's two great books, His special revelation (the Bible) and His general revelation (creation). He spoke of the scientific enterprise as studying the book of God's works. Because Bacon laid the foundation for how scientists think, he's been called the "Father of the Scientific Method." The path he left for us is built on what's called inductive reasoning, which includes observation, hypothesizing, and experimentation. Those three components have guided science for nearly four centuries.

Let's compare deduction and induction, the two ways of reasoning that we all use. Deduction follows this pattern: (1) Conclusions are drawn *before* examining the experience. (2) It then reasons from that general conclusion to the particulars. (3) It works from the cause to the effect. And (4) it yields *necessary* conclusions, that is, conclusions that must be true if the premises are true and the form of argument is valid.

Inductive reasoning flows in the opposite direction: (1) Conclusions are drawn *after* examining the experience. (2) It reasons from the particulars to the general. (3) It works from the observed effect back to the cause. And (4) it yields only *probable* conclusions, that is, the conclusions are not necessarily true in the deductive sense, but more or less likely to be true. In this inductive or scientific method, the observed effects are analyzed to form hypotheses about causes, which lead to theories that explain the data.

Let's describe the separate steps. The scientist first gathers data by watching related phenomena. Like Sherlock Holmes, the scientist eyes everything in detail so that he might solve "the crime." Careful observation helps him form a hypothesis that he hopes will prove accurate. In this hypothesizing stage he forms a possible reason, an educated guess, for the way things work in the case being studied. It states what the examiner thinks is going on so that he can test the hypothesis. Finally, he conducts an experiment to see whether or not the hypothesis is true. If the predictions turn out as expected, this suggests that the hypothesis is true as well. The observations, hypotheses, and predictions come together in the experiment in which the scientist's educated guess is confirmed or disconfirmed.

All scientific theories are tentative. Since they are often revised, Christians shouldn't jump on the scientific "bandwagon" too quickly when science supports a Christian doctrine. In time, a dominant scientific view may be replaced by a new theory that contradicts Christian teaching.

The scientific method is possible because our universe is ordered and understandable, and effects arise from prior causes. Those features are part of created reality which reflects an orderly, intelligent Designer—the God of the Bible. We can credit the possibility of science to the good, wise, and powerful God who created us and our world, and intends us to study it so we might glorify Him.

Is There a Philosophy Behind Science?

SCIENCE **54**

Some atheists claim that science is omnipotent. They believe it's the only avenue by which we discover truth. But far from being all-powerful, science is limited, based on assumptions not provable by the scientific method.

First, science assumes external reality, independent of the mind, that can be studied and known. External reality exhibits order and design that make it understandable. Without this, the scientific endeavor would be meaningless. Christians understand that the universe displays order and design because the Creator built them into His creation. Without that knowable, understandable external reality, science could not exist.

Second, science assumes the law of cause and effect. Everything that begins to exist has a cause. This law is foundational for the scientific enterprise, but it cannot be proven by the scientific method. Christians believe that the universe exhibits this tendency because God designed it that way. A world without this trait would be chaotic and dangerous. We wouldn't know what would happen as the result of various causes. For instance, when we heated water we couldn't know if it would boil at 212 degrees or 50, possibly causing serious injury.

Third, science assumes the uniformity of nature, meaning that the present is like the past, and the future will be the same. Certain things in the natural world remain consistent. To use the previous example, the temperature at which water boils will be the same tomorrow as today and yesterday. Nature is uniform because God made it that way.

Christians and science alike affirm these assumptions as undeniable and self-evident. But science doesn't possess the ability to prove everything and yield comprehensive truth. *First*, it cannot prove the laws of logic, which govern all thought and action. They are built into the fabric of the universe, and originate in the nature of God. Even though the scientist can't prove them, she must use them for the scientific method to be possible.

Second, science cannot prove objective moral values. Some thoughts, words, and actions are right and others wrong, but science can't demonstrate that. The scientist himself adheres to ethical standards in his work such as honesty, but he can't prove that honesty is a virtue. Absolute moral standards find their origin in the transcendent, unchanging God. They are revealed by Him rather than discovered by science.

Third, ironically, science cannot prove the scientific method. This doesn't mean the method is fatally flawed, but that it can't be demonstrated as the only way to find truth. Science is a useful, legitimate means by which truth about the world can be discovered, but it does operate on several assumptions and is limited in scope.

Christians should be aware of science and its limitations. The Bible and science never truly contradict one another. Since the universe is the work of God's hands, and the Bible is His disclosure of Himself, the two always agree. Our interpretations of God's Word (the Bible) and His works (Creation) are capable of error. When a contradiction arises between science and the Bible, it reflects our faulty understanding. No conflict exists between nature and the Bible because both originate in the One who is all-knowing, all-powerful, and incapable of error.

The Worldview Behind Science

55 | SCIENCE

As we've seen, a worldview is a system of belief about ultimate reality. Each worldview begins with assumptions—beliefs that are accepted as true without considering if they could be false. These assumptions are not necessarily bad if they're recognized. But when they're not, they often lead to intellectual blindness and faulty conclusions. Much of science is guided by the worldview of naturalism—the belief that nature is the only thing that's real. The physical universe and the laws that determine its behavior are all that exist. Nothing supernatural, including God, exists, or if it does, it cannot intervene into our physical world.

When the prevailing assumption is naturalism, everything in that culture, from law to journalism to education, reflects and reinforces that premise. Naturalism, then, determines the ultimate story of truth, that culture's explanatory myth. God resides only in religious peoples' imagination—and these people are seen as irrational, even dangerous, because they may be seen as a threat to the cultural myth. Naturalism thus becomes its own religion with a built-in incentive for self-preservation and dominance.

Today, from grammar school to the university, naturalism is the mandatory assumption of nearly all disciplines. Starting from that unexplored foundation, the results of almost all research will, of course, support only naturalistic conclusions. As an illustration, if the only answer allowed to the following question is "red," what answer will we get when we ask, "What color is the [green] chalkboard?" "Red," because every other possible answer has been ruled off limits from the start. This process is obviously flawed, but if the rules have been preset, some of the answers, including at times the correct answers, are preeliminated.

Naturalism is the basic assumption for Darwin's theory of evolution. There is no hard scientific evidence to support naturalism, but Darwinists hold it tenaciously, because their myth of naturalism gives them cultural influence, even dominance. To let go of naturalism would allow opposing points of view that might threaten that influence. They are often more concerned with protecting the myth than they are with genuine scientific investigation. And since they set the rules of the game, they do so to protect their myth—nothing else is taken seriously. So the assumption of naturalism establishes a monopoly on truth for Darwinists.

As an assumption, naturalism is philosophy, not science. It's based on faith, not on evidence found by research. And when naturalism masquerades as science it often leads to bad science. It can hinder the legitimate search for truth because it denies the possibility of answers outside itself. It's bad philosophy as well because it cannot answer such fundamental questions as "Why is there something rather than nothing?" And, "Why is this assumption, rather than a different assumption, the only legitimate place to begin?"

So when naturalists label Christians "religious fanatics," we might question their own rationality. Those who protect their myth by refusing to explore all the evidence may be less rational than Christians.

Has Science Made Christianity Irrelevant?

Some people believe that science and Christianity oppose one another. That view arises from two myths: (1) Science disproves Christianity; and (2) Christianity has persecuted scientists whose discoveries challenged the church's opinions.

Let's respond to these challenges in order. Some cynics claim that science has disproved biblical statements about nature. For example, the Bible, it is claimed, teaches that the earth is flat. Since science has proven that the earth is a sphere, science disproves the Bible, right? No, because the verses in question don't teach a flat earth. Passages that mention the corners of the earth, the ends of the earth, or the foundation of the earth are figurative language. We talk like this today. A speaker at a large conference might say that people have come from the corners of the earth, but we don't accuse him of believing the earth is flat. We recognize his figurative language—he's saying people have come from everywhere. Neither should we say that science disproves the Bible because it uses such language.

Other verses use observational language, describing things as they appear in everyday life. For instance, the Bible speaks of the sun rising and setting. But how can anyone honestly accuse the Bible of scientific inaccuracy because of that? Scientifically trained meteorologists use such language, and no one faults them. Terms like "sunrise" and "sunset" are everyday terms, not meant to be scientifically precise phrases. To fault the Bible for using everyday language to describe nature is hypocrisy.

What about Christianity's alleged oppression of scientists? In some of its less enlightened moments, the church did persecute scientists such as Galileo. On the other hand, most historians have persuasively argued that Christianity actually provided the environment from which modern science arose. Some even say Christianity was the primary cause of science. Whatever the exact historical relationship between the two, their alleged conflict is not supported by the evidence. Christianity portrayed the universe as separate and distinct from the mind, complete with structure and order, and therefore understandable. That perspective was needed for science to begin and then develop. This conceptual framework is supported by the fact that many of the greatest scientists were theists, even Christians.[5]

A second consideration is that some of this country's most prestigious universities were established by Christians, including Harvard, Yale, and Princeton. Christianity promoted the highest level of scholarship because it believed in the value of seeking truth in both God's Word (the Bible) and God's works (creation). Christianity and science were seen as part of the same enterprise—finding truth. New England Puritans believed that no activity, especially the act of learning, was meaningless if life was lived in awareness of God.

To say that science disproves Christianity misunderstands both. Far from making Christianity irrelevant, science owes its very existence to the worldview of an ordered, knowable, understandable universe that reflects a Creator.

Introducing the Origins Debate

The 1960 movie *Inherit the Wind* was a fictional story of the 1925 Scopes Trial, known as the "Monkey Trial." The film has proven to be effective propaganda depicting evolutionists as reasonable, witty, and virtuous, and creationists as bigoted, anti-intellectual buffoons. Even today, the image of Christians is unknowingly filtered through the *Inherit the Wind* grid. This debate over origins is vitally important. We'll introduce four key issues: (1) the doctrinal necessity of creation; (2) the ethical impact of creation; (3) the difference between operation science and origin science; and (4) the distinction between microevolution and macroevolution.

First, creation lies near the center of Christian theology, raising questions about other essential doctrines. For example, if Adam was not literally created by God, did the human race experience a literal fall? If not, do we need atonement? If man is not in a sinful state, why did the Son of God become incarnate, live a sinless life, and die for our sins? Those core Christian doctrines are meaningless without a literal creation.

Second, the origins debate influences ethics. For instance, if humans resulted from evolution, why would we possess any rights over other species? In addition, the evolution viewpoint could imply that certain races are more or less developed than others, and therefore, superior or inferior. Hitler would love that one. Marriage would not be a special relationship, but merely a social-biological convention for perpetuating the human species. The question of origins affects all those issues.

Third, operation science and origin science must be distinguished. The first deals with regular, observable patterns. Origin science, on the other hand, is more forensic, related to unrepeatable past events like the beginning of the universe. Much as a forensic scientist tries to reconstruct a crime scene by examining evidence, so origin science seeks to understand what happened in the past. Evolutionists explain the beginning and development of life by natural processes; creationists explain it as the work of a supernatural Designer. But both creationism and evolutionary theory are origin science.

Fourth, note the difference between macroevolution and microevolution. The first believes that *all life and all species of life* came from a single ancestor, or small number of ancestors, which arose from nonliving matter. Microevolution refers only to change *within a species*—a fact with which creationists agree. Evolutionists see the evidence for microevolution and infer macroevolution as a result, even though evidence is lacking to support that conclusion.

Molecular biologist and medical doctor Michael Denton addresses the issue, as seen in this edited summary: "The supremacy of the evolutionary myth has created an illusion that evolutionary theory was proved one hundred years ago and that all research since then has supported it. Nothing could be further from the truth. In fact, the evidence was so patchy one hundred years ago that even Darwin had increasing doubts about his view. The only aspect of his theory that's been supported is where it applies to microevolution. His general theory is still highly speculative. It has no direct factual support."[6]

Intelligent Design Theory

Prior to Darwin, theologians, scientists, and philosophers admitted that nature pointed to a Designer. With the advent of Darwinism, some scientists began to pose natural explanations for the design they saw in the universe. But that trend must now compete with the scientific movement known as "Intelligent Design." Its proponents are biologists, biochemists, anthropologists, physicists, astrophysicists, astronomers, philosophers, and mathematicians.[7] They believe that the origin and fine-tuning of the universe, as well as the diversity and complexity of life, have been designed, and that this design is scientifically detectable.

Some critics charge intelligent design with the old "God of the gaps" thinking. In those arguments, God was the answer for everything when a natural explanation wasn't found. But intelligent design theory is not based on what we *don't* know but what we *do* know about the universe and life within it. Because the universe and life reveal signs that only intelligence produces, a Designer is the only plausible conclusion.

Consider the analogy of wind and water erosion on stone. At times, by chance, shapes that resemble people result. But erosion cannot account for the faces on Mt. Rushmore—faces of real men. Those shapes do not reveal the marks of erosion. The effect on Rushmore is complex (angles and milling marks) and specified (an end result was in mind). Chance is ruled out by the specified complexity, which comes only from an intelligent source.

The intelligent design movement claims that the apparent design in the universe is not just apparent, but real, like that on Rushmore—the result of intelligent purpose. If chance is ruled out, and intelligent design proposed as the cause of the faces on Rushmore, the same conclusion can be drawn for life and the universe. They're both far more specific and complex than one mountain.

Evolutionists say we can't verify design in nature. Two responses: *First*, if that's true, the same can be said for archaeology. Imagine criticizing an archaeologist who suggests an intelligent source behind ancient cave paintings. He does so because he knows through analogy that painters (intelligent causes) produce paintings.

Second, a favorite program of some scientists, including many evolutionists, is SETI (Search for

Extraterrestrial Intelligence). That research is built on the belief that design is noticeable. SETI scientists know that a message from space sent by intelligent beings would look different from other signals because it would bear signs of design made by an intelligent source. If that makes SETI reasonable science, then intelligent design is reasonable for the universe and life as well. The criticisms of design theory fail under scrutiny and are inconsistent with the acceptance of other scientific programs. Intelligent design theory is here to stay.

Is Design Theory Science?

Where does life come from? Is it the product of natural descent—gradual development from the forces of nature? Or does it come from intelligent design—the deliberate product of a knowing Agent? In recent decades more and more scientists have accepted intelligent design as a plausible option. Committed evolutionists, however, rely solely on natural processes to explain life. They say that design theory doesn't possess the defining marks of science and is therefore not a legitimate answer. Let's introduce three of their arguments and then reconsider the basic question.

One objection is that design theories don't appeal to natural law. But that charge limits the possible options, maybe even the right one. It demands a certain kind of conclusion before the evidence is considered. An honest search can't rule out any potential result before it begins. Also, whatever happened at the beginning of the universe is nonrecurring. It doesn't happen again. That presents a problem for natural theories, such as descent, because they're based on observing repeated patterns.

59 SCIENCE

Because whatever did happen can't be repeated, natural law can't be used to discover why and how it happened. Design theory is no less scientific than descent theory because both try to explain nonrepeatable, historical events.

A second argument against design theory as science is that it doesn't explain; it only describes. But many natural laws do the same. For instance, the law of gravity merely describes a regular event. It doesn't explain why gravity is there in the first place. Natural law doesn't get behind the "Why?" question any more than design does.

Another argument against design as science is that it includes unobservable things, such as intelligent cause or even God. But science does the same. For example, theoretical physics accepts many things that can't be directly seen: forces, fields, atoms, and quarks. Other unobservables incorporated in scientific study are mental states, molecular biological structures, and past events. Evolutionists, who criticize design theory for this reason, are guilty of the same. They continually tell us that evolution occurs at rates too slow to observe. So both kinds of theories use unobservable things in their arguments. If this is a fatal flaw for design theory then it must be for descent theory also.

From the other direction, there is evidence that intelligent design theory is science. In all of life, the past actions of an intelligent designer leave noticeable effects in the present. For example, if a person stumbles upon a painting that exhibits form, and purpose, and planning, and design, we infer an intelligent source as the cause. We reason that a painter did this, and we're right. That's a legitimate conclusion based on the observable *result* of intelligent design, even though the designer is now not seen by us.

But the whole discussion about whether or not intelligent design theory is scientific misses the real issue. The concern should not be if something is *scientific*, but if it's *true*. That underlying fact, however, is often lost in the debate, especially among Darwinists. Too often, the wrong question is being asked. It's not, "Which kind of theory is scientific?" but simply, "What happened?"

Did the Universe Begin?

SCIENCE 60

Astronomer Carl Sagan used to say, "The cosmos is all that is or was or ever will be." According to Sagan, the cosmos had no beginning, needed no *Beginner*, and will never end. Sagan's view contrasts with the Bible, which teaches that the cosmos began, the result of a personal Creator: "In the beginning God created the heavens and the earth" (Genesis 1:1).

One argument for God's existence is based on the assumption that the universe had a beginning. First developed by medieval Islamic philosophers and now used by Dr. William Lane Craig, the *Kalam* Cosmological Argument goes like this:

Premise (1): Everything that begins to exist has a cause.

Premise (2): The universe began to exist.

Conclusion: Therefore, the universe has a cause of its existence.

Premise (1) affirms the undeniable law of causality. But what about Premise (2)? Let's consider arguments (one philosophical; two scientific[8]) which demonstrate that the universe is not eternal but began to exist a finite amount of time ago. *First*, the philosophical argument:

Premise (1): If an infinite number of moments occurred before today, then today would never have come because it's impossible to pass through an infinite number of moments.

Premise (2): Today has come.

Conclusion: Therefore, there must have been only a finite number of moments before today, thus showing that the universe had a beginning.

A *second* argument relates to the second law of thermodynamics, which states that the amount of usable energy in a closed system is running down (becoming more disordered). But if the universe is both eternal and "running down," this leads to the contradiction that the universe has been in a constant state of running down, and yet, has not done so. If the universe is getting more and more disordered, it can't be eternal, or it would be completely disordered by now, which it's not. Therefore, the universe must be finite in duration.

The *third* argument deals with the expansion of the galaxies. Scientific evidence testifies that the universe is not in a holding pattern. It's not static but is expanding outward from a central point. This leads to the conclusion that the universe *began* from a single point.

The field of astrophysics confirms that the universe came from nothing. Christian theologians and philosophers call this creation *ex nihilo,* "out of nothing." This means there was nothing, then there was something. In the first century BC, Roman philosopher Lucretius asked the most basic question of all, "Why is there something rather than nothing?" In other words, why did the universe begin to exist?

The universe must have a cause. Its beginning from nothing had to come about by means of something else. That cause must be spaceless and timeless, because space and time began with the universe. Furthermore, that first cause must be eternal and without cause itself because an infinite series of causes is impossible. The universe itself cannot be its own cause because it's temporal, changing, finite, and had a beginning. It would seem that this spaceless, timeless, eternal cause draws us back to Genesis 1:1, *"In the beginning God . . . "*

Is It Soup Yet?[9]

Charles Darwin suggested that life began in a "warm little pond" that contained the necessary chemicals and atmospheric conditions. This "prebiological" evolution seeks to describe how life originated and developed from nonliving chemicals. Much research since Darwin's time has been devoted to the subject, but the evidence doesn't support his suggestion.

In the 1950s, graduate student Stanley Miller took a course on the origin of the solar system taught by Nobel laureate Harold Urey. Miller responded to Urey's challenge to simulate the earth's early atmosphere while passing energy through it. He put ammonia, methane, and hydrogen in a sealed, glass container of hot water, and then simulated lightning with a spark. In a few days the water and glass were stained with reddish goo containing amino acids—the building blocks of protein, the basic "stuff" of life. The experiment seemed to provide evidence that life could arise from chemical reactions in Darwin's "warm little pond."[10]

Let's consider three related facts. *First*, the "warm

61

SCIENCE

little pond" probably didn't exist. Evidence indicates that the early earth was laid to waste by meteorites and comets. A growing consensus of scientists doubts that the atmosphere contained significant amounts of ammonia, methane, or hydrogen. In other words, conditions were not favorable for so-called primordial soup possibilities. Miller-type experiments do not mimic the conditions of the early earth.

Second, human involvement nullifies any similarity between Miller's exercise and the early earth. When conducting an experiment the scientist makes choices that would not be present in the original conditions. So there's a vast difference between the formation of life's building blocks in the prebiotic soup without intelligent guidance, and the modern experiment where things are intentionally crafted to produce that result. The comparison is wrong.

Third, protein production is essentially an information problem. Getting all the building blocks (amino acids), and in the proper sequence, requires information or instructions. This is known as *specified complexity*. Consider this illustration: A newspaper is complex—it has many symbols (letters). It's also specified—the symbols must come in proper sequence to form words, sentences, paragraphs, and articles. To be meaningful, the paper must exhibit both complexity and specificity. The production of functioning proteins also requires specified complexity.

The odds against life's origin by natural means are huge. Astrophysicist Sir Fredrick Hoyle stated, "The current scenario of the origin of life is about as likely as the assemblage of a 747 by a tornado whirling through a junkyard."[11] Sir Francis Crick (Nobel laureate scientist best known as one of the discoverers of DNA) exclaimed, "The origin of life appears to be almost a miracle, so many are the conditions which would have had to be satisfied to get it going."[12] Rather than admit that possible miracle, Crick proposed that life was "shipped" to earth by an ancient, extraterrestrial civilization, a suggestion that exposes the bias against supernaturalism.

From Aardvarks to Zebras

Why is life so diverse? Why are there trees, flowers, algae, and mold; beetles, spiders, snails, and flies; sharks, dolphins, whales, and squid; lions, leopards, cows, and apes; and humans? For over a century the dominant answer within the scientific community has been macroevolution: the view that all life started with a single-celled organism and developed and diverged along an "evolutionary tree." This evolution, millions of years in the making, is guided by natural processes, causing life to branch into new organisms and groups of organisms.

But a worthy challenge to that answer has arisen from intelligent design. We should consider it for two reasons: (1) Intelligent design provides as much explanation as macroevolution does for the vast diversity of life. (2) It accounts for things that macroevolution cannot, such as the complexity of life, the integration of organisms to function for a purpose, and the mind. Let's explore these reasons.

1. Supporters of macroevolution argue their view

from alleged similarities between organisms. Because of those similarities, they say, organisms are related, part of the same evolutionary tree. But organisms are made up of millions or billions of features. From that enormous number we would expect widespread similarity in the major necessities of life such as respiratory systems and skeletal systems. But many species, in fact, have very different systems. If evolution were true, why that difference? Also, organisms share atomic and subatomic similarities even to rocks and gases, but that doesn't indicate genetic connection between living and nonliving things.

And we would expect some similarities in creatures made by intelligent design. Similarities appear even in the products of human intelligence as a result of common purposes and common materials. For instance, all cars have an engine, wheels, and a steering device as a result of their common purpose. They likewise all include glass, metal, and plastic as a result of the basic stuff from which they're made. Those similarities suggest a common designer (the human mind) not a relationship between the cars. The similarity among organisms can be understood as the work of a Creator who fashioned things for the same purpose—life—and used the same basic stuff of the universe to make them.

2. Intelligent design accounts for things that macroevolution does not. First, the amazing complexity of life is unanswered by macroevolution. Those complexities defy a purely natural explanation. Second, macroevolution cannot account for integration—for example, how an organism's complexity works for a purpose, the organism's function. If things are out of place the organism and its various parts won't work well, if at all. Finally, macroevolution cannot account for the mind. According to all natural theories, everything is matter or inseparable from it. But even though our minds are connected with our brains, they are immaterial.

Intelligent design explains some things better and accounts for others that macroevolution does not at all. Intelligent design offers a more plausible account for the diversity of life's major groups.

Only the Strong Survive

Before Charles Darwin's time, men speculated that life evolved, but Darwin proposed a mechanism that explained how. His book *The Origin of Species* argued three crucial ideas. *First*, new species have appeared throughout history by natural means. He called this "descent with modification." *Second*, evolutionary processes can account for the diversity of life because all living things had descended from one or just a few microscopic ancestors. And, *third*, the process was guided by natural selection or "survival of the fittest."

Natural selection refers to the mechanism by which some characteristics of an organism make it more suitable to survive and pass on its genes to its offspring. That's not controversial. It makes sense that only the most fit live to pass on their genes. Weak and helpless offspring with defects rarely survive to sexual maturity to be able to reproduce. But Darwinists claim that the same process has the ability for a single cell to result in billions of descendants ranging from trees and flowers, to spiders and birds, and humans.

This speculation is built on the power of mutation. Mutations are random genetic changes that are usually harmful. Occasionally they may slightly improve the organism's ability to survive, and that rare beneficial effect may be passed on to some offspring. As the process continues, the trait may eventually spread to the entire species. Allowing enough time for successive changes, whole new organisms might emerge. This scenario is where the controversy lies. It suffers two major problems.

The *first* is misinterpretation of the so-called evidence. Consider the evolutionists' example of peppered moths during the industrial revolution. It is claimed that this example confirms natural selection, and they are right. Dark moths had a greater chance of survival because trees were darkened by industrial smoke, camouflaging the darker moths from predators. When the trees became lighter due to better air quality, the lighter moths had the advantage. The fundamental question, however, is not if this supports natural selection, but if it demonstrates that natural selection reproduces new species. It does not. No evidence points to new species, new organs, or other major changes. The moths remained moths even when exhibiting variations. Minor variations within a species are not evidence of macroevolutionary change.

A *second* problem is their false analogy. Darwinists say that practices like dog breeding support their view on natural selection. Since many variations can be produced by interbreeding dogs, then over billions of years even more variation could result from mutation and natural selection. But two different concepts are being compared: *natural* selection and *artificial* selection. One is not guided by intelligence while the other is. Furthermore, even with intelligent guidance permeating the selection process, the uniform result is always a dog, never a cat, a fish, or any other animal. This point actually demonstrates the *limits* of variation within a species.

Because evolutionists automatically rule out any supernatural involvement, they're committed to finding only a natural explanation. Thus that's all they will find despite the lack of evidence for their conclusions.

Darwin's Theory Mutates

When scientists speak of mutation they refer to genetic change, the result of random errors in copying the DNA's genetic code. Even though mutations are usually harmful, evolutionists theorize that in a few cases they prove beneficial.[15] If the mutations are favorable, then the change will "take hold" through natural selection. Over time successive mutations can produce complex organs and new types of biological life.

Darwin's contribution was a mechanism that produced this change. His theory of small, accumulated mutations over a very long time didn't need sudden leaps producing new organisms in one generation. That was a miracle or supernatural intervention that would contradict his philosophy of materialism. So he explained how biological change came about over long periods of time by natural processes—mutation and natural selection.

The fundamental question is whether or not these tiny changes, even over a long time, can actually do what Darwin and others claim. They cannot! *First,* complex organs such as the eye cannot be produced by gradual evolution. What good would a partial eye provide? Part of an eye is different from partial vision. All of the components of an eye must be present for vision to occur. So select components of an eye offer no evolutionary advantage. Eyes and other complex organs and biological systems can't be developed through chance mutations. And Darwin knew that his theory would break down if complex organs could not be accounted for by "numerous, successive, slight modifications."[16]

Second, Darwinists make a false inference—namely, since mutation is indispensable, and since macromutation has been ruled out, successive micromutations *must* be the answer. That's faulty reasoning. The impossibility of a theory at one end of the mutation scale is not evidence for the theory at the other end of the scale. But Darwinists are committed to naturalism, so they're compelled to find something that "works" despite the lack of evidence.

Third, the ability of micromutation and natural selection to produce vast biological diversity and complexity seems mathematically impossible. It depends on several factors: (1) the number of favorable micromutations required to create complex organs and organisms; (2) the frequency of these micromutations when and where they're needed; (3) the ability of natural selection to preserve such benefits with enough success for them to accumulate; and (4) significant time allowed by the fossil record for this to happen.[17] When mathematicians have calculated the probability of Darwinian evolution based on these criteria, they conclude that it's essentially impossible. But evolutionists react by asserting that the calculations are flawed. They again reveal their unwillingness to reconsider their theory in light of the evidence as well as their unwavering commitment to their philosophy of naturalism.

The Fossils Speak, but What Do They Say?

Do only scientific illiterates doubt evolution? Hardly. In the early nineteenth century French scientist Cuvier, the father of paleontology, concluded that the geological record showed no trace of evolutionary development. Later in that century, fossil experts, not theologians, were Darwin's main opponents. Since that time, the fossil record has been explored in much greater detail, but the expected gradual evolutionary picture has never emerged.

Considering the lack of transitional forms among the fossils, Darwin asked, "why, if species have descended from other species by [very] fine gradations, do we not everywhere see innumerable transitional forms?"[18] He concluded that the lack of fossil evidence was "the most obvious and gravest objection . . . against my theory." That fact led the most respected paleontologists and geologists to unanimously and strongly believe that species remained unchanged.[19]

213

Darwin and others pointed out that few fossil beds had been researched. They believed that when more beds were discovered and examined, the record would demonstrate his theory. But they were wrong. The late Harvard paleontologist Stephen Jay Gould admitted the failure of evidence for Darwinian gradualism: "The extreme rarity of transitional forms in the fossil record persists as the trade secret of paleontology. The evolutionary trees that adorn our textbooks have data only at the tips and nodes of their branches; *the rest is inference*, however reasonable, not the evidence of fossils"[20] (emphasis added).

The fossil record is inconsistent with gradual development of species in two ways: (1) When most species appear in the record, they look much the same as when they later disappear; and (2) In any given area, a particular species does not arise gradually by steady transformation, but appears fully formed. Both facts are the opposite of what Darwin predicted. Examination of the fossil records in the world's best fossil beds has not yielded a single transition from one species to another. The fossil record simply does not support Darwinian evolution.

Niles Eldredge, world-class fossil expert, summarizes the failure of the fossil record to support gradual development of species: "No wonder paleontologists shied away from evolution for so long. It never seems to happen. Assiduous collecting [of samples] . . . yields . . . minor oscillations, and the very occasional slight accumulation of change—over millions of years, at a rate too slow to account for all the prodigious change that has occurred in evolutionary history. When we do see the introduction of evolutionary novelty, it usually shows up with a bang, and often with no firm evidence that the fossils did not evolve elsewhere! Evolution cannot forever be going on somewhere else. Yet that's how the fossil record has struck many a forlorn paleontologist looking to learn something about evolution."[21] Even the world's greatest evolutionary scientists know the theory has a problem.

Still Missing After All These Years

Much has been made about finding the "missing link." Since evolutionists believe that humans evolved, we too must have an ancestral tree. So our development should be observable in the fossil record. But it's not. No discoveries reveal human evolution. But that hasn't stopped the claims of having found the "missing link." Three bear mentioning.

In 1922 a tooth was discovered in Nebraska, which led to the introduction of "Nebraska man." From this tooth alone, an entire ancient Cornhusker was constructed. But the tooth was later discovered to be from a wild pig, not a human ancestor. How a single tooth, a pig's tooth at that, could be used to construct a missing link raises questions about the whole process.

Another proposed missing link is "Java Man," discovered on the island of Java in 1891. He consists of a skullcap, a femur, and three teeth. Furthermore, the femur was found a year later and fifty feet away from the skull cap. Perhaps most unsettling is that the discoverer, Eugene Dubois, said little about the two human skulls found nearby. Too many uncertainties surround Java Man to consider him evidence of human evolution.

Those supposed missing links were stupid mistakes. Piltdown man, however, was a deliberate fraud,[22] one of history's greatest scientific hoaxes. The jaw of an ape was stained to match the color of a human skull, and other bones were reshaped as well as stained. Although Piltdown Man was later proven a hoax, two highly esteemed paleoanthropologists, Sir Arthur Keith and A. S. Woodward, said that Piltdown man "represents more closely than any human form yet discovered the common ancestor from which both the Neanderthal and modern types have been derived."[23] Most disturbing, Piltdown man was used for decades to portray human evolution as a fact to students.[24]

Two observations: *First*, evolutionary paleontologists and others assume human evolution to be a fact, and then interpret their findings in light of this "fact." A better procedure is to let discoveries guide the conclusions. *Second*, the study of human origins has been awash with subjectivity more than almost any other branch of science. At least three factors make it so: (1) Since Darwin, the descent of man from lesser developed ancestors has been considered certain within the culture of evolutionary scientists, (2) instant worldwide fame would accompany the discovery of a genuine missing link, and (3) extreme pressure to confirm human evolution via the discovery of missing links drives the process.

Museums are notorious for constructing humanlike displays which they label truth and fact. Whole scenarios of prehuman ancestors are pictured to give the impression that much is known about human evolution. But that's not true. Given museums' influence on public opinion, it's no wonder that the myth of human evolution has become ingrained in the culture's thinking. But human origins research has not yielded evidence that would compel a sensible person to embrace human evolution.

The Sum of the Parts

Most of us operate a computer, but few understand how it works. Even with the cover removed to reveal its insides we see no connection between its parts and what they do. The computer may be called a "black box," a term for a device that does something but whose workings remain a mystery.

Some people think that evolution solved all the biological black boxes, but that's not true. Darwin couldn't explain how eyes see, how blood clots, how the body fights disease, or many other functions. But he understood one thing—these black boxes could prove his theory false: "If it could be demonstrated that any complex organ existed which could not possibly have been formed by numerous, successive, slight modifications, my theory would absolutely break down."[25] He unknowingly announced his theory's death sentence.

Enter *irreducible complexity*. This refers to any system of interacting parts that needs every part to function. The removal of even one of the parts will cause the system to stop functioning. Dr. Michael J. Behe, professor of biochemistry at Lehigh University, writes, "An irreducibly complex system cannot be produced . . . by slight, successive modifications of a [previous] system, because any [previous system] to an irreducibly complex system that is missing a part is by definition nonfunctional. An irreducibly complex biological system . . . would be a powerful challenge to Darwinian evolution."[26]

A mousetrap is irreducibly complex. If even one part is missing, it won't work. The device consists of a base; a hammer to pin the mouse to the base; a spring to press against the base and the hammer when the trap is charged; a catch that releases when pressure is applied; and a bar that connects to the catch and holds the hammer back when the trap is charged.[27] The system is irreducibly complex—it requires all five parts to function.

The bacterial flagellum, which allows many bacteria to swim, is a tiny propeller rotated by a motor. It requires all its parts to function.[28] Many similar systems exist. Behe concludes, "No one . . . can give a detailed account of how the cilium, or vision, or blood clotting, or any complex biochemical process might have developed in a Darwinian fashion."[29]

The irreducible complexity of biological black boxes, which confounds Darwinian evolution, argues for intelligent design. Behe concludes that, "The result of . . .

efforts to investigate the cell . . . at the molecular level . . . cries *'design!'* The result is so unambiguous and so significant that it must be ranked as one of the greatest achievements in the history of science. The discovery rivals those of Newton and Einstein."[30]

From Shrewsbury to the World

Charles Robert Darwin (1809-1882) was the son of a physician born in Shrewsbury, England. His name is synonymous with the theory of evolution, but what made his theory unique was not his contending that evolution took place. Others had said that. Darwin's notoriety arose from his proposal of a natural mechanism whereby evolutionary change could occur. By applying natural selection (survival of the fittest) to variations within populations, Darwin argued that small changes could accumulate, leading to the origin of new species without intervention of a guiding intelligence.

His life is a microcosm of the growing disbelief of the eighteenth century. He started as a theist, believing in an all-powerful, all-knowing, all-good Creator who was responsible for the diversity and complexity of life. In 1828, he entered Cambridge where, consistent with his father's desires, he prepared for the ministry. But during that time he began to question Christianity. Just as the broader culture grew antitheistic, so did Darwin.

The defining event of his life was the now famous voyage aboard the *Beagle* (1836) in which he conducted groundbreaking biological research. Prior to his voyage, possibly as late as 1835, Darwin remained a creationist. But about this time his belief in the Bible's scientific accuracy began to wane as he embraced the antisupernaturalism argued for by philosophers Benedict de Spinoza and David Hume. Darwin concluded that it was highly unlikely that miracles ever occurred or were even possible.

His greatest objection to Christianity may be what he called the "damnable doctrine" of hell.[31] He thought Christianity inconceivable because of its conception of a God who eternally separates people from Himself in hell. The final impetus for his unbelief may have been the death of his daughter Anne in 1851. Darwin was deeply grieved and angered. By the time Anne died, his views on evolution had solidified. His monumental work *On the Origin of Species* was published in 1859.

Darwin denied being an atheist but he remained an agnostic until his death in 1882. Some Christians have propagated the myth that Darwin was converted to Christ on his deathbed. But the evidence of history does not confirm that. And it would prove nothing about his theory even if he had converted to Christianity and recanted his evolutionary views. Evolution stands or falls based upon whether or not it's true. No theories are true or false because of who believes or rejects them, but rather are based on their correspondence to the way things really are.

Charles Darwin was one of the most influential people of recent centuries. The evolution of beliefs in his own life exemplify the natural theory he is famous for. His shift from theism to agnosticism paralleled the cultural shift away from theistic belief to growing unbelief. In many ways, he lives on through the antitheistic, evolutionary speculation of many of today's scientists.

Do the Heavens Declare the Glory Of God?

Creation reveals a beauty and complexity that eclipse anything man can make or imagine. It also tells something about the Creator: "The heavens declare the glory of God; the skies proclaim the work of his hands" (Psalm 19:1). If the universe is the product of God's creative hand, we would expect to see His "fingerprints" stamped across it, and we do. What the Bible said centuries ago is being noted by some of the world's foremost astronomers.

First, the elements needed for life argue for design. Carbon forms only if it possesses a precise level of a nuclear property called "resonance." This notion of resonance includes the collision of helium nuclei, leading to the formation of carbon. The slightest variation of energy levels would not allow carbon to form, or would instantly destroy it. Conditions had to be perfect to make this basic building block of life. When considering the probability of such fine-tuning, the late astrophysicist Sir

Fred Hoyle, credited for the discovery of the resonances of carbon and oxygen atoms, commented that it was virtually impossible that such resonances exist by chance. He concluded that atheism was greatly shaken because of this discovery.[32]

Second, the ratio of proton to electron mass confirms that the universe was designed. The proton is 1,836 times heavier than the electron. Scientists don't know why. But they do know that if that ratio were much different, crucial life-building molecules wouldn't form, and there would be no chemistry and no life. The precise ratio of proton to electron mass appears to be deliberate to pave the way for life. Physicist Stephen Hawking says, "The remarkable fact is that the values of these numbers seem to have been very finely adjusted to make possible the development of life."[33]

Third, the relative strengths of nature's four fundamental forces (gravity, electromagnetism, and the strong and weak nuclear forces) appear to have been perfectly balanced to permit a life-sustaining universe. If even one of the four had a slightly different strength, such a universe would be impossible. Scientists have concluded that this precision can be accounted for only by a Designer's guidance. Physicist Edward Kolb states, "It turns out that 'constants of nature,' such as the strength of gravity, have exactly the values that allow stars and planets to form. . . . The universe, it seems, is fine-tuned to let life and consciousness flower."[34]

Related to the remarkable precision of the universe, agnostic astronomer Robert Jastrow comments, "Astronomers now find that they have painted themselves into a corner because they have proven, by their own methods, that the world began abruptly in an act of creation. . . . And they have found that all this happened as a product of forces they cannot hope to discover."[35] Modern astronomy is confirming what Paul wrote to the Roman Christians, "For since the creation of the world God's invisible qualities—his eternal power and divine nature—have been clearly seen, being understood from what has been made" (Romans 1:20).

Could Complex Speech and Abstract Thought Have Evolved?

You may not like courses in grammar and English, but consider your capacity to learn and use language to create and communicate thoughts. You possess thousands of words and the grammatical tools from which to assemble those linguistic units into meaningful statements. What accounts for that? Is human language ability only an elaborate system of animal cries—a short step beyond gorillas' and chimps' communication skills? Are human beings just animals with better vocal systems, or are we creatures made in the image of God who reflect His traits, including the ability to think and speak with language? Can human language capacity be accounted for by evolution, or is it the result of intelligent design?

Most research in this field tries to show that human language is merely an extension of animals' abilities. More specifically, the studies address the question of whether or not apes can acquire human language systems. Even though apes can indeed develop a fairly large vocabulary of symbols that correspond to real situations, the overall answer seems to be "no." They cannot engage in human linguistic behaviors such as abstract thought, a distinguishing mark of human language and a characteristic of true rationality and intelligence.

This means that apes cannot think through hypothetical scenarios or reflect upon what might have been or might happen. For example, an ape cannot ponder and respond to an abstract possibility such as the following: "If I were to drop the cup on the floor it would break; so I won't drop it." Nor is there convincing evidence that apes can independently, without human coaching, form and ask real questions—questions that do not merely express a desire. Compare that with a child who learns at a very young age what a question is and, without prompting, asks them often.

Unlike apes, humans have an *infinitely* expandable vocabulary. Human children acquire a rich vocabulary so flexible that they can create and combine words for almost anything. And apes achieve only about 80 percent accuracy using signs, whereas children rarely misapply a sign to a situation. According to one prominent linguist, claiming that any prehuman's first primitive cry was the initial step toward language is like saying that the first animal to climb a tree took the first essential step in exploring outer space.[36] Quite a stretch.

The "verbal behavior" of trained apes fails to demonstrate that human language is only a more developed form of animals' abilities. Humans' capacity for abstract thought and reflection is unique. And if it did not evolve from the primal cries of animals into complex statements with vocabulary and grammar, where did it originate? Apparently it was implanted within us as part of the image of a rational, communicating God.

The Supernatural Calling Card

Extremism rules the world of opinion about miracles as it does about many topics. Some people deny the possibility of miracles; others obsess over alleged supernatural events. Miracles appear throughout the pages of Scripture, usually to validate God's spokesmen. The prophets, Jesus, and His apostles were confirmed by signs and wonders. Their extraordinary acts testified that they spoke for God—He was the source and inspiration of their message. Without the supernatural "calling card" of miracles, these men might have been rejected more than they were.

We might define miracles as acts of God that interrupt or bypass the natural order. They can be a suspension of natural laws like the sun standing still (the earth ceasing to rotate, Joshua 10:13). In those cases, God temporarily "turns off" the laws of the universe. Or they may be the result of a greater force superseding a lesser force. For instance, the clothes of Shadrach, Meshach,

71

MIRACLES

231

and Abednego didn't burn because the fireproof hand of God shrouded them from the flames (Daniel 3:22-26).

Atheists reject the possibility of miracles simply because they disbelieve in God. It makes no sense to speak of God acting in a supernatural way if He's not there at all. If nature is everything, it operates according to its own unchanging laws. Since all events must be explained by those laws, miracles are ruled out by definition: no supernatural realm, no supernatural acts. Classical apologetics, therefore, seeks first to establish God's reality. Miracles become possible if God exists because the One who could create a universe would be able to intervene into His work any way He wanted.

The deist's argument against miracles starts differently from the atheist's but ends the same. They believe in a supernatural Being who created the universe, but deny that He interferes with the world He made. His creation operates according to fixed laws, and He doesn't tinker with what He set up. He created, then withdrew, leaving the world to run entirely on its own. So miracles are just as impossible for the deist as for the atheist.

We offer three responses to the arguments against miracles: (1) The skeptics beg the question. Given their worldview of naturalism, they predefine miracles as impossible—which is the very point of debate. In other words, they draw their conclusion before they investigate. (2) All research should be done according to the methods appropriate for the subject. Miracles fall outside the procedures used for examining natural events. Therefore, the methods demanded by a naturalistic worldview are the wrong tools for that search. And (3) They operate with a flawed view of natural law, which doesn't tell us what *must* happen, but describes what usually *does* happen. In other words, the laws of the universe are *descriptions,* not *prescriptions.*

The fundamental question is, does a God exist who can intervene into the world? If He's not there, miracles indeed seem impossible. On the other hand, if a theistic universe is established, miracles become possible and actual. In the end, the issue is God, not miracles.

God's Special Intervention

Finding balance is always a challenge, and this search for balance applies to our view of miracles. On the one hand, skeptics deny the possibility of miracles under any conditions. On the other hand, some people believe they occur regularly. Various religions claim supernatural events; followers of the occult conjure up demonic powers; some Christians allege miraculous healings at nearly every church service they attend. These competing claims make it hard to define and verify miracles. How can we know that a particular event is a miracle, and how do we identify its source?

Some paranormal events can be attributed to natural causes like the power of suggestion, sleight of hand, or simple deception. Others may be truly supernatural—the work of demons. But only God, the maker of heaven and earth, can perform true miracles. According to that understanding, the following would not properly be called miracles: demonic activity, supposed miracles in other religions, or predictions from astrology or horoscopes.

But how do we know a supernatural event is the work of God or demons? The Bible is the standard. It helps us distinguish between true and counterfeit miracles, true and false prophets, acts of God and Satan. The key is distinguishing between miracles and magic.[37] A miracle is God's intervention into the created order, whereas magic is man's manipulation of creation by means of normal or paranormal powers.

Miracles occur by God's control, are not available upon human command, support what is good and true, and affirm Jesus as God in the flesh. Magic results from man's control, is available on command, supports evil and error, and denies that Jesus is God in the flesh. Applying those criteria helps us evaluate supernatural events. For instance, if someone performs amazing acts but denies that Jesus is God's Son, his works don't come from God. If someone stages paranormal feats that are condemned by Scripture, God is not the source.

Genuine miracles are also superior to the counterfeit. When Elijah confronted the prophets of Baal, the superiority of God was seen in fire from heaven that swallowed the altar and water (1 Kings 18). No one can compare to Jesus' healing the sick, restoring sight to the blind, and raising the dead (Matthew 4:24; Mark 10:51-52; John 12:1,9). Finally, biblical prophecy is precise and accurate, unlike the vague and often wrong predictions of astrology. Christ predicted His own betrayal (Matthew 26:21), His death (Mark 8:31), the way in which He would die (Matthew 16:21), and how long He would be in the grave before His resurrection (Matthew 12:39-40).

While Christians believe God performs miracles, we must not be deceived by every supernatural claim today. We can evaluate reports of the miraculous according to Scripture. Miraculous acts of God can be identified as such by applying biblical principles. We should heed Jesus' advice to be as wise as serpents, but as innocent as doves (Matthew 10:16).

When Is a Miracle Not a Miracle?

Modern society holds inconsistent views about the supernatural. On the one hand, people believe horoscopes, palm-readings, and psychic hotlines that saturate our culture. On the other hand, Christians are considered gullible because they believe the miracles recorded in the Bible.

One famous objection to miracles arises from Scottish philosopher David Hume (1711-1776). He believed that a wise person bases his belief on evidence gathered by the senses, our means of obtaining knowledge. Our experience, perceived by our senses, tells us that the world operates according to unchanging natural laws. A miracle, as defined by Hume, violates those unalterable principles. Events that seem miraculous contradict our past experience that says nature is uniform. Therefore, we should reject the claim of miracles, and explain them by natural law. "I was apparently mistaken or deceived about what I thought was a miracle."

73 MIRACLES

237

Likewise, when someone tells us of a miraculous event, the wise person should ask which is more likely: that the witness lied or was deceived, or that nature's laws were violated? We shouldn't believe that a miracle occurred until evidence indicates that it's more likely that natural law was violated than that the witness lied or was mistaken.

The evidence does not prove, however, that nature's laws are never violated. Yes, the laws of nature are the norm. But just because things *do* happen a certain way *most* of the time doesn't mean they *must* happen that way *all* the time. More factors count as evidence when a miracle is in question. The integrity of the witness, the event itself, alternate explanations, and the framework from which the event is viewed all contribute to understanding what happened.

According to Hume's criterion, miracles could never be supported by evidence. He doesn't really weigh the evidence, but counts the frequency of events and considers the statistics an argument against miraculous claims. But, it's just not that simple. For example, apply Hume's criterion to Christ's resurrection. Since death happens to everyone, and there are very few resurrection claims, Christ's resurrection should be rejected. It's not credible because nonresurrection is observed more often. But that procedure misses the point. The issue is not if resurrection happens *often*, but if it happened *once*.

If we follow Hume's approach, no events that might have happened just once or very infrequently could be true. Even events that are known to be true would have to be judged as not possible. For example, someone who won the lottery should not believe they won because millions who play never win. But the winner did win. Being dealt a perfect bridge hand is not possible because the odds are 1,635,013,559,600 to 1. But it has happened.

Counting stats doesn't determine the reality of miracles. They are rare by their very nature. If they happened often, we wouldn't call them miracles. They become possible and credible when we view life from a Christian worldview, seeing the universe as the work of an infinite, personal Creator.

The Source of Miracle Reports

Some people say miracles are myth, primitive thinking about unreal gods and demons acting in our midst. They represent a prescientific way of thinking that contradicts the modern mind. Therefore, enlightened thinkers reject accounts of miracles.

C. S. Lewis, professor of medieval and renaissance literature at Oxford and Cambridge, was recognized as a world expert on myths. And he knew that the Gospel accounts, miracles included, did not exhibit the marks of mythology. He believed that the miracles of mythology displayed a disjointed, absurd universe, completely inconsistent with the reality we know. Christian miracles, however, even though supernatural, fit the universe as it is. The miracles of the Bible don't match the traits of mythology—they are different.

Theologian Rudolf Bultmann (1884-1976), known for his *demythologizing* method of Bible interpretation, believed that all miracle accounts were mythological. His conclusions influence people to this day. For instance, some say that Christ rose from the dead, but not in a real, physical way—only as a subjective reality for the believer who chooses to believe that. It wouldn't matter if Jesus' corpse was found because such subjective faith is not based on objective facts. Contrast that with Paul who wrote that if Christ isn't raised from the dead (a physical resurrection in space and time), the believer's hope is in vain (1 Corinthians 15:17).

People may believe that the biblical miracles are myths because they believe that the Bible is only a religious storybook of moral lessons. But the Bible describes events that really happened in space and time and points to One who controls world affairs. It portrays miracles as real—supernatural ways in which God operates—not mythological stories. If the God of the Bible is real, then miracles are possible. Therefore our quest about the reality of miracles should begin with God's existence and the nature of the Bible as His Word before considering the reality of the miracles contained within its pages.

Much of the issue about miracles focuses on the Gospels. Some say they can't be trusted as reliable history precisely because they contain miracle stories. That view is based on the assumption that miracles are not possible. But that begs the question. The one who concludes this needs to step back and reconsider if her naturalist worldview is true. The nature of miracles can't be dealt with objectively unless one's worldview assumptions are honestly acknowledged and examined.

Some anti-Christian skeptics dismiss the miracle accounts in the Gospels because they include theological information. But that conclusion reflects obvious bias. The Gospels are full of theological implications, but that doesn't undermine their ability to accurately record historical events. If we set aside antitheological prejudice, the Gospels bear the marks of straightforward history.

Are miracles myth? It depends on one's starting point. If God exists and the Bible is His Word, then miracles occurred in real time-space history. The Bible does not allow us to assert otherwise with any sort of integrity.

Applying the Right Test

Miracles are God's intervention into the natural world—His special work for a specific purpose. Originating from the One who created natural laws, miracles are not bound by those laws, but transcend them. Science tries to uncover the regular processes that govern the universe. It seeks to discover the laws that explain normal events in our world. Therefore, science examines observable, repeatable, predictable patterns in nature. Because of that, miracles can't be classified as scientific.

But how important is that? If miracles aren't scientific, are they therefore false? The real issue is not if something is scientific, but if it's true. But naturalistic scientists often miss the point by how they frame the question. They consider science the only route to knowledge, rejecting as false or irrelevant anything outside that realm. They limit the possibilities of truth to categories they preselect. In the process, science assumes many things it cannot prove: the laws of logic, the uniformity of nature, the scientific method itself. So the fact that miracles don't lend themselves to scientific inquiry does not argue against their truth.

Science is great, but the scientific method is simply the wrong criterion for judging miracles. By their nature as unique, one-time events, they don't lend themselves to observability, repeatability, and predictability. So they shouldn't be evaluated by those standards. We don't give a math test to students in an English class and then flunk them in English for failing the math test! The test or criterion must fit the situation, and applying the scientific method to miracles doesn't fit.

In one sense, miracles are not completely unscientific. As the work of an intelligent cause, their effects can be observed. We look at the product of a *someone* rather than a *something* and conclude that it was designed, not the result of chance. The principle can be noted in the Mt. Rushmore illustration. Think how unreasonable it would be to explain the faces on Rushmore as the result of natural forces when they display obvious evidence pointing to an intelligent cause. Likewise, when we evaluate events like healing a blind man or Christ's resurrection, a supernatural cause is fully rational, but a naturalistic one makes no sense.

Miracles and the phenomena studied by science are two different categories. Therefore, if we ask, "Are miracles scientific?" meaning discoverable by scientific methods, the answer is "no." Miracles are unique, non-uniform events, endowed with purpose by God. Science, however, strives to understand events that are governed by nonpurposeful, natural law. Miracles, by definition, are exceptions to those laws. Thus miracles and the events investigated by science require separate explanations.

Falling outside the realm of science does not render miracles false. They are simply not a source of scientific knowledge as found through scientific procedures. Even though miracles are not scientific as defined by science, belief in them is reasonable, and they can still be true. To think otherwise exposes a bias that is itself not based on science, but on philosophical assumptions. And because science cannot prove those assumptions, consistency would exclude the scientist from adhering to his own position.

Did Miracles Really Happen?

Some people believe miracles are scientifically feasible, but they reject them as history. In other words, miracles could happen, but never have. So they say the Bible's accounts of miracles are false. Consider, for example, the resurrection of Christ. Christians accept it as a real, space-time, historical event, the foundation of our faith. But according to those who reject the historical reality of miracles, it never happened.

The view that miracles are unhistorical is based on the belief that the present is the key to unlocking the past. The way things operate now is the way they've always worked. This argument applies the principle of uniformity, similar to that found in the natural sciences, to the study of history. Because miracles are not observed now, they never occurred before. So the biblical record of miracles must be explained by something else, perhaps myths or hallucinations or deceptions incorporated into the biblical text centuries later.

Two errors surface in this argument: (1) Who says miracles are not observed today? Such a contention can't be demonstrated; it assumes what can't be proven. Miracles may not be the norm today, certainly not as common as when God gave special revelation, but a biblical view of history doesn't require God to act the same way at all times. Even if miracles are not now observed, that has no bearing on their possible occurrence in the past. And (2), the principle of uniformity is not even applicable. By its very nature it doesn't apply to singular events such as miracles. If they occurred repetitively, they wouldn't be miracles. So discounting them because they don't happen often is highly irrational.

Let's reconsider the Resurrection. The consensus of New Testament scholars is that the following four events are historical facts: (1) Jesus' death on the cross, (2) His burial in the tomb of Joseph of Arimathea, (3) the empty tomb, and (4) Jesus' post-resurrection appearances. Those events really happened, but they need interpretation. The question is, "What explanation best accounts for those facts when seen together?" Based on the evidence, Christians believe the Resurrection is the most reasonable conclusion. The skeptic finds himself in the awkward position of having to offer a naturalistic account for an event that falls outside nature's bounds, and the evidence says so. Ironically, he ruled out the most likely conclusion before he began his investigation.

This argument exposes its own error—rejecting a possible answer before the evidence is even examined. The notion that the past must be understood by the present is unreasonable in this case because miracles, by nature, are rare. As with other topics in this section, worldview assumptions set the stage for final conclusions. And those who doubt the historical reality of miracles make assumptions like Christians and everyone else. The naturalist's assumptions leave him with no viable alternates. The Christian's assumptions lead to a rational, consistent conclusion—if God exists and the Bible is His Word, miracles are historical.

Christianity's Wellspring

Christians revere Judaism as the wellspring from which our own faith was born. We believe that Christianity fulfills rather than replaces Judaism. It all started 2,000 years before Christ, when God chose Abraham to be the father of many people (Genesis 12:1-3). Today almost 14,000,000 Jews claim Abraham as their ancestor, but being Jewish by race does not automatically make one Jewish by religion.

Two generations after Abraham, his family moved to Egypt during a famine. Their descendants were later enslaved by the Egyptians, then liberated by Moses in the Exodus about 1450 BC. While traveling to the Promised Land, Moses received God's Law, the Torah, the first five books of the Bible. Israel was then led by judges until they cried for a king, which God game them in Saul, David, and Solomon in the eleventh and tenth centuries BC. After Solomon, the kingdom was split into Israel in the north and Judah in the south. Israel was taken captive by the Assyrians in 722 BC, and Judah by the Babylonians in 586 BC. The Persians then conquered

Babylon, and Cyrus allowed the Jews to return to their own land and rebuild their Temple. They eventually came under Rome's control, and in AD 70 the Romans destroyed Jerusalem and the second temple, stopping the sacrifices and priesthood, and scattering the Jews.

Until two centuries ago, the only form of Judaism was what is now called "Orthodox Judaism." They follow the Mosaic Law and the old ways passed down from their ancestors. But during the eighteenth century, some Jews adopted European ideas and practices. The central concern of this "Reformed Judaism" is ethical application, often taken from the prophets. A middle position, known as "Conservative Judaism," arose in the nineteenth century. They blend into modern culture but maintain at least parts of the Law.

The Jewish Bible is the Christians' Old Testament. Not all Jews consider it inspired, but almost all deeply respect it. They divide it into three sections: the Law, the Prophets, and the Writings. Many Jews give a higher place to the Law than the rest of Scripture. They also accept the Talmud, a collection of legal rulings, traditions, and interpretations of the Torah.

The central belief of Judaism is the unity of God from Deuteronomy 6:4: "Hear, O Israel: The LORD our God, the LORD is one." Most Jews have replaced the ancient belief in a personal Messiah with the hope of a coming age of justice. Most consider obeying the Law and doing good deeds more important than beliefs. Many observe some or all Jewish holidays, which recall their special history, and observe ceremonies to mark major stages of life: circumcision at birth, *bar mitzvah* for boys and *bat mitzvah* for girls at age thirteen, as well as marriage and funerals.

Because of the Jews' heritage as the foundation of our faith, Christian interaction with Jews is unique. Knowing which branch of Judaism a particular Jew adheres to can aid efforts to share the good news of the Messiah. As a result of centuries of anti-Semitism, which came in part from Christianity, Jews may be understandably cautious. Sensitivity is required, but when a trusting relationship is built, we can explain that following Jesus does not mean abandoning their Jewish heritage. He is the Messiah for all people.

In Allah's Name

Interest in Islam skyrocketed after September 11, 2001. People were amazed that anyone could do such evil in the name of religion. But since the ultimate value in Islam is submission, a *Muslim,* "one who submits," will do whatever he or she is convinced that Allah (God) wants. Almost 20 percent of the world's population adheres to Islam, second only to Christianity.

Muhammad's religion began with his teachings in the seventh century. When he was forty he suffered convulsions, during which he claimed to receive visions from the angel Gabriel. He first thought these visions came from demons, but his wife convinced him they were divine. Their content, including monotheistic teaching, was eventually recorded as the *Qur'an.* When he taught this to the polytheists of Mecca, they forced him and his followers to flee in 622. Muhammad and his followers went to war for the next ten years to gain converts and land, and in 630 they recaptured Mecca.

Muhammad died without appointing a successor. His followers differed over how to pick one: some wanted to elect his replacement; others favored one from his bloodline. The dispute led to two groups: Shi'tes and Sunnis. The Sunnis won the debate and now make up over 80 percent of Islam.

Muslims believe that God revealed Himself in some of the Jewish Scriptures and in the Christian Gospels, but they think the Christian Bible is now corrupted. Gabriel's revelation to Muhammad, compiled in 114 chapters of the *Qur'an*, is the Word of Allah, which is perfect in the original Arabic.

The five pillars of Islamic belief are: (1) God is one, Allah. (2) God has sent many prophets, including Abraham, Moses, and Jesus; of these, Muhammad is the last and greatest. (3) The gap between God and man is filled with angels, some good, some evil. (4) The *Qur'an* is the highest book, above the writings of other prophets. (5) We will all stand before Allah on judgment day, when our eternal destiny will be determined by our deeds.

Faithful Muslims do the following: They repeat their central belief that "there is no God but Allah, and Muhammad is his messenger"; pray five times a day while facing Mecca; fast during daylight hours in the ninth lunar month (Ramadan); give at least 2 ½ percent of their wealth to the poor; and make a pilgrimage to Mecca once in their lifetime.

The God of Islam is not the Christian God. They are both sovereign, omnipotent Creators and Judges of the world. But the Christian concept of tri-unity is the ultimate blasphemy to Muslims. Furthermore, unlike the Christian God, Allah is distant, lacks or hides his love, motivates by fear, and acts arbitrarily if he wants to.

Many Muslims enter America through our university system. Twenty percent of the half million foreign students on our campuses are from Islamic lands. After graduation many return home, but others stay. By showing love and respect, we can talk with them about Jesus, whom they consider to be a prophet. Most Muslims who come to Christ do so through a Christian friendship. Islam may be the most serious challenge to Christianity in today's world, but God's grace reaches them too. Our gentle portrayal of a personal relationship with a loving God offers a life Muslims don't have, but many want.

Gentle Intolerance

Baha'i is one of the world's newest religions, a nineteenth century spin-off of Islam. Six million people from almost every country and culture follow it. That broad base is fitting for a religion that promotes universal peace, brotherhood, and oneness as the foundation of its teachings.

Like today, nineteenth-century Islam was not known for tolerating different views. But a Persian Muslim named Miza' Ali Muhammad (known by his followers as the "Bab," which meant the "gate" to paradise) claimed to be a greater prophet than Muhammad and all others. He taught that the world's religious leaders had deviated from their origins—the belief in the unity of all things. As a result, the Bab was murdered in 1850 for "heresy." But his followers maintained his teaching that a Messiah of sorts, "a Promised One," would someday come to unite mankind. In 1863, the Bab's successor, Mirza Husyn' Ali (known as "Baha'u'llah") claimed to be this manifestation of the one true God. His followers were called Baha'is.

Like Islam, Baha'i is strictly monotheistic, denying the Trinity. But they believe that God has sent a prophet for every age (Abraham, Krishna, Moses, Zoroaster, Buddha, Jesus, Muhammad, the Bab, Baha'u'llah), each replacing his predecessor. They were all divine, sinless manifestations of God, and each of their religions succeeded the old one with updated truth. The wise person, therefore, latches onto the latest and greatest, the final prophet—Baha'u'llah.

The unifying theme of Baha'i is oneness—all people, religions, and science are one at heart. But all their talk about equality and unity only applies within their own religious and political world. As the capstone of this universal thrust, everyone should live under the jurisdiction of a world court. All people and nations would be subject to the Baha'i governing council, which would sovereignly rule over all.

Believers in Baha'i respect the Bible as they do the sacred books of all religions. But their true authority resides in the writings of Baha'u'llah. While in prison, he wrote almost 200 books and tablets, which followers consider absolute truth. Jesus is given a prime place in Baha'i literature that is used in predominantly Christian countries. But Jesus' role as prophet of His age ended when Muhammad succeeded him in AD 622. The Baha'i faith denies Christ's deity and rejects His atoning death and resurrection.

Christians who meet Baha'is are often impressed by their knowledge, gentleness, and concern for world problems. They usually portray themselves as Christians because in their mind they follow every religion. But Christians should remember that Baha'i tolerance for Christianity is deliberately designed to appeal to them. The content of core Christian doctrine is gutted—only an empty shell of meaningless words remains. Their respect for and use of the Bible is calculated to convince gullible people that Baha'i is "Christian." In reality they use the Bible to draw Christians into their fold as they use other religions' Scriptures to do the same thing.

Upon deeper inspection, this gentle, inclusive religion turns out to be as exclusive as other religions. If we scratch the surface of Baha'i, we find a faith diametrically opposed to Christianity. A basic understanding of Baha'i, seen from a biblical foundation, will guard the Christian from falling into this deceptive religion.

It's Not About Zoro

Zoroastrianism is not the worship of Zoro, but a religion founded by Zoroaster, who lived about 600 BC. It claims only 200,000 adherents today, but it dominated ancient Persia prior to the Islamic conquests in the seventh century AD. It still exists in Iran, India, and other places where immigrants have brought it.

At the age of thirty, Zoroaster claimed to receive a vision from an archangel. He laid aside his body and entered the presence of God who told him to teach monotheism to those who worshiped many gods. Zoroaster obeyed and taught the existence of one true god who alone should be worshiped. Zoroaster's teaching was largely rejected until the king converted to his views a decade later. After that, as with most religions, variations developed, especially a tendency toward dualism—belief in two equal, competing gods, one good, one evil. Orthodox Zoroastrians viewed that as heresy, but the idea spread.

Over the next two centuries, Zoroaster's monotheism was further compromised by people accepting gods from the Persian Pantheon, including the god Mithra. Roman soldiers eventually spread the cult of Mithra across parts of their Empire. In the third century AD, a prophet named Mani associated this dualism with matter (evil) and spirit (good). Spirit was trapped within matter and yearned to be free to return to God, its source. Manichaeism became influential across the Roman Empire, counting among its followers the great theologian Augustine before his conversion to Christianity. For a thousand years, from the third century BC until the seventh century AD, Zoroastrianism was the official state religion of Persia.

The dualistic tension between a good god and an evil god is what Zoroastrianism is known for today. The evil spirit will eventually lose the cosmic war, but each person chooses good or bad deeds in support of these competing powers. One's eternal destiny is based on those choices. Over time, ritual purity from ceremonial acts to guard against evil spirits became more important than moral decisions. Like many religions, Zoroastrianism practices symbolic rituals at the four major stages of life: birth, puberty, marriage, and death.

During the early twentieth century, scholars who believed most religions were related and evolved from one another gave Zoroastrianism an important place in the development of Judaism, Christianity, and Islam. But that view was based on assumptions that could not be verified, so it's less common today. Furthermore, the alleged similarities between Zoroastrianism and other religions are less real than they first appear. And what influence there was may have gone in the other direction, from Judaism to Zoroastrianism during the Jews' captivity in Persia before Cyrus released them.

Many modern Zoroastrians emphasize their ethnic identity and culture more than their religion. Since most have accepted a pluralistic mindset, Christians can relate the gospel to them as they would to others who think many paths lead to God. We can agree with those who believe in the cosmic battle between good and evil. But the final victory over evil has been won. We can tell them of the liberating news of Jesus' crucifixion and resurrection victory over Satan.

The Heart of India

Seven hundred million people, mostly in India, are Hindus. About one million now live in America. One of the world's oldest religions, Hinduism is a collection of mostly pantheistic ideas. Its complexity and fluid belief system have generated three other religions: Jainism, Buddhism, and Sikhism.

Almost 2,000 years before Christ, the tribal peoples of northern India practiced an occultic, polytheistic religion. Over time their simple rituals became more elaborate, requiring priests to execute them properly. Eventually this priestly class grew distant from the common people and became the only way to approach the gods. A rift finally occurred between the priests and people, resulting in a religion that stressed individual, internal meditation.

The oldest Hindu scriptures are the *Vedas*. This collection of hymns and prayers was first transmitted orally. To ensure that the priests would always know how to do their rituals, the *Vedas* were preserved in writing over a thousand year period beginning about

81 | HISTORIC RELIGIONS

1400 BC. The *Upanishads,* the last part of the *Vedas,* were written between 800 BC and 300 BC to record secret teachings, including the idea that behind the many gods is one ultimate reality, *Brahman.* A less authoritative but more popular scripture is the *Bhagavad-Gita* from the first century AD. Due to Hinduism's complex belief system, many sects and subgroups evolved, including some that are more theistic than pantheistic, like Hare Krishna. As a consequence of such diversity, no unifying creed or doctrinal statement exists, resulting in tolerance of nearly all views. Apparent contradictions among Hindu sects or other religions don't bother the person enlightened by Hindu wisdom because she believes that a greater unity lies behind these discrepancies.

Despite these various groups and their diverse ideas, several core beliefs are common. First, God and the universe are one—the ultimate, impersonal reality, *Brahman,* is everything. All distinctions in what we think we see or claim to know are *maya,* illusion. Even our true, inner self, *atman,* is one with *Brahman.* We are bound to the law of karma which says we receive the results of our actions in the next life. Thus we're trapped in the repeating cycle of reincarnation. Our souls experience liberation from this revolving wheel of rebirths by transcending the illusion of distinctions and recognizing the oneness of all things, including that we are God.

Salvation is earned in one of three ways: (1) *Works* of ritual, fasting, and sacrifice that yield good karma. (2) *Knowledge* achieved through discipline and meditation on the sacred writings leading to a state of consciousness beyond the law of karma. (3) *Devotion* to one of the Hindu deities harmonizing the devotee with that deity.

Hindus tolerate other religions because they see them as one. So they may be happy to add Jesus to their list of gods. The Christian's challenge is to convey Jesus' uniqueness and His message of forgiveness. Living under the law of karma, Hindus struggle to understand forgiveness by the impersonal *Brahman*. But if we present God as personal and offended by our sin, forgiveness becomes more feasible. Like everyone else, Hindus understand forgiveness in human relationships, and a personal God gets closer to that reality in their lives. Only Jesus can free them from the cycle of rebirths striving to work off their karmic debt.

A Hindu/Muslim Mix

Hindu and Muslim tensions have led to a long and sometimes bloody history on the Indian subcontinent. A fifteenth-century effort to resolve the conflict resulted in a new religion, Sikhism, which claims twenty million adherents today. Sikhs believe, however, that they are more than a synthesis of their two parent religions; they claim to be a new faith with new revelation.

A thousand years ago, northwest India was ruled by a militant form of Islam. Over the next few centuries, Hindu reformers taught new doctrines that increased people's acceptance of different ideas, and in the fifteenth century a respected poet preached that all people should unify their religions. Under the influence of his ideas, another Hindu named Nanak claimed a revelation from God commissioning him to modify Hinduism by including elements of Islam.

For the next 200 years the new movement, eventually known as Sikhism, was led by a succession of ten gurus. In response to relentless persecution, the Sikhs gravitated away from their pacifist teachings toward a more militant stance. By the time of the tenth guru, Gobind Rai, Sikhism had almost become a quasi-military system. He announced that he was the last guru before his life was taken by a Muslin assassin.

Their scriptures are called the "Illustrious Book," or the "Original Book," or the "Lord's Book." Its hymns and poetry were gathered or written by various gurus, several of whom claimed divine inspiration. With the death of Gobind Rai, authority passed to that book, which is kept in the Golden Temple in Amristar, India. Six languages were used in its writing, making it unreadable by all but a few. Despite that hindrance, believers hold it in such high regard that they are sometimes accused of idolatry.

Sikh beliefs are a mix of Muslin and Hindu views. Like Muslims, they are monotheistic, believing in one sovereign but impersonal God who is beyond understanding, originally known simply as the "True Name." Like Hindus, they believe in karma and reincarnation, which they escape by devotion to God conveyed through chanting and singing hymns. As they understand the divine order of the universe they come into harmony with it, eventually experiencing union with God's light.

This harmony of salvation is sought by internal devotion rather than external ritual. The seeker engages in meditation, submitting to the divine Name by repeating a sacred word or syllable. The process occurs over stages until the soul is mystically merged with God. New Sikhs are initiated into full fellowship by a baptism of sorts—drinking holy water in the name of the gurus. At their temples they worship by chanting from their Scriptures, then sharing a meal that even visitors may join in as a symbol of the equality of all people.

Sikhism offers no compelling vision of the future other than a vague hope of uniting mankind in a religion of universal brotherhood. They don't anticipate a grand culmination such as a coming Messiah or a final kingdom. Christians find a point of contact with Sikhs by offering a definite future hope—a returning Messiah who revealed God long before any gurus appeared. Individual, conscious salvation is available from a personal God who gives hope for the future and eternity.

We Wouldn't Hurt a Fly

Mahatma Gandhi's ideas on politics and economics, society and passive resistance, were partly based on Jainism. This small but influential religion began as a reformation movement within Hinduism during the fifth century BC, but it shares some beliefs with Buddhism. Most of its five million followers live in India, and are known for asceticism and nonviolence.

Jainism was founded by Mahavira, a title meaning the "great man." His early life and some of his teachings so parallel his contemporary, Gautama (the Buddha), that some scholars believe they influenced each other. When Mahavira was about thirty, he rejected his life of luxury and vowed to pursue extreme asceticism, neglecting even the most basic physical needs. According to Jain tradition, he wandered in silence and meditation for twelve years without clothing or shelter, seeking his soul's liberation.

The enlightenment he achieved was a form of omniscience whereby he understood the universe and everything in it. He was liberated from the law of karma and

83 HISTORIC RELIGIONS

released from the cycle of reincarnation. He had become a *jina*, "conqueror," from which the name Jain comes. Jains are therefore "those who follow the conqueror," or "those who overcome." Mahavira is the teacher of our age, even though Jains believe he was the last of twenty-four such conquerors, also called *Tirthankaras.*

Some of the Jain scriptures originated from Mahavira's sermons. His listeners orally transmitted his truths to future generations until a council of monks established their canon of Scripture about 300 BC. They were finally recorded in writing in the fifth century AD, but followers still debate which books are authoritative.

Jainism believes that all living things—plants, animals, and humans—possess a soul. Like Hinduism, they accept karma and reincarnation, although they think each soul remains distinct and never absorbs into Brahman. Living a good or bad life adds or removes physical bits of karmic matter to the soul, determining one's station of life after rebirth. They also reject belief in any god, other than Mahavira, whom they now worship. He and the twenty-three other *Tirthankaras* possess divine-like powers that followers seek and use to aid them in life. At the practical level, they follow three guiding principles: no absolutes in thought or speech, efficiency of actions, and nonviolence toward all life.

Jains practice ascetic self-denial and complete harmlessness, by which they hope to gain liberation. Monks must adopt the strictest form of asceticism; laypeople follow less stringent demands, focusing more on rituals. They avoid passions like anger or actions that could arise from such passions. Few of them work jobs that require manual labor like farming for fear they might unintentionally kill a tiny living creature. Most pursue harmless occupations like finance or business. Because of their honesty and efficiency they often do well.

Jainism is one of the most legalistic religions on earth, and its extreme view of not harming any life can lead to despair. The most cautious person kills microorganisms in the air and water just by living life. But no means of salvation is available other than to do better, thus shedding the karmic build-up on the soul. In relating to Jains, Christians first need to convey an infinite but personal God. We can then offer grace to counter the deadening effect of hopeless works. Sin can be and is forgiven by God because His Son paid the price to satisfy divine wrath.

The "Enlightened One"

During the last generation, Buddhism has become popular in the West. It originated in India five hundred years before Christ when Siddhartha Gautama opposed the Hindu caste system and some of the Hindu Scriptures. Over 300 million people worldwide claim to be Buddhists, representing a wide variety of beliefs and practices.

Gautama was born about 560 BC. His wealthy father sheltered him from the hardships of life, but in his twenties he was exposed to the sickness, poverty, and old age that haunt most people's lives. As a result, he abandoned his life of luxury to try to eliminate suffering. He studied Hindu masters and pursued an austere lifestyle, but concluded that asceticism was as empty as luxury. So he chose the middle path of meditation, achieving enlightenment while meditating under a tree. He thus became the source of truth for other seekers, the Buddha—a title meaning "enlightened one."

In the third century BC Buddhism split over who could achieve enlightenment and what to include in Scripture.

Theravada Buddhism says only the most committed may find enlightenment. Mahayana Buddhism believes that all can achieve that blessed state. Concerning Scripture, Theravada closed its canon after the *Tripitaka*, "The Three Baskets," teachings from a narrow range of sources including Buddha, even though his ideas were not written down until 400 years after he died. Mahayana includes many other writings, as many as 5,000 volumes, from sources in India, China, Japan, and Tibet.

Buddhists believe that desire leads to suffering. The solution is found by attaining a selfless outlook on life, achieved through the Four Noble Truths: (1) Life is suffering; (2) Suffering comes from desire; (3) Eliminating desire conquers suffering; (4) Desire is removed by following the Eightfold Path of right understanding, thought, speech, action, livelihood, effort, awareness, and meditation. Pursuing this path, and therefore doing away with desire and suffering, removes the illusion that the self exists. We thus reach nirvana—the ultimate state after deliverance from the cycle of rebirths.

The most familiar form of Buddhism in the West is Zen, a variation of Mahayana. Its roots are found in China about AD 400, and it includes elements of Taoism. "Zen" is more than a name; it's a concept for all that is.

It's an expression of monism that claims to be beyond distinctions or categories; the absolute beyond description or thought, including life and the experience of life. Zen is Mind, and humans are simply a manifestation of Mind. A disciplined life delivers us from a sense of self, helping us transcend dualistic ideas. Salvation, nirvana, is inner awareness of our oneness with all that is.

Christian and Buddhist discussion can begin from several shared values such as: the danger of excess desire that leads to suffering, the need to live a moral life, and the value of self-discipline, prayer, meditation, and compassion. Then we can point out the difference between Buddha and Jesus, whom they recognize as a spiritual Master. Jesus claimed to be the only means of eternal rest, delivering us from the desires of life and the suffering that results. In effect, He paid our karmic debt by His death. Christians already experience a degree of eternal peace, which is available for all, including Buddhists.

Following the Sage

Confucianism refers to the social and political system of ethics credited to Confucius about 500 BC. This collection of wise sayings is not a religion—it addresses man's relationship with each other more than with God. As many as 1.5 billion people in China, Japan, Korea, and Vietnam follow these ideals.

In 551 BC Confucius was born into a noble but poor family in the state of Lu in China. He lived during a time of chaos as Chinese feudalism had collapsed into near anarchy; the country was in desperate need of an ethic to guide culture and politics. In his late teens, he began a government career consisting of several minor posts. By the age of fifty, he had risen to prime minister of Lu, but resigned a few years later in a dispute over the ruler's policies.

For the next thirteen years he traveled from state to state sharing his wisdom with feudal rulers, hoping to establish peace and security. But his views were largely rejected, and he lived his last five years back in Lu, teaching and writing his ideas—now considered clas-

85 HISTORIC RELIGIONS

sics. Over the centuries, his thoughts were gradually accepted and incorporated into Chinese culture, and his followers elevated his stature to that of a god.

The second sage of Confucianism is Mencius—born in 371 BC when the social fabric of China was no better than during Confucius' time. His career paralleled his master's, even being rejected by the leaders of his day. He then devoted himself to teaching and developed the view of mankind's inborn goodness, a central Confucian belief even now.

Confucius is credited with writing many of China's ancient books, including some he probably did not write. The accepted canon of his works—largely commentaries on previous writings, edited further by his followers—includes the *Five Classics* and the *Four Books*. These are collections of poetry, history, and wisdom sayings.

The Confucian worldview does not begin with God but with an ultimate reality called "Heaven," the impersonal foundation behind our world. Mankind should live by Heaven's mandate, the moral order within nature. Humans are innately good, and commit evil only when influenced by outside forces. Through self-improvement and compliance with the standards of culture, we improve our goodness to the benefit of society.

The rules for conduct are summarized in six guiding

principles: (1) Humaneness, or seeking others' good; (2) Relating to people with propriety in all circumstances; (3) Being a true gentleman; (4) Acting one's part; (5) Using power responsibly; (6) Pursuing peaceful arts such as music and poetry. Few would disagree with those guidelines. If everyone would obey them, any society would be much better.

But ethics without God works only if mankind really is good by nature. And neither Confucius or Mencius gave sufficient evidence to overcome the verdict of history that mankind is not basically good. Christianity provides a better explanation and offers hope for eternity. We were indeed created good, but something changed that, resulting in massive problems. We have fallen through the sin of the first pair. But a personal God made it possible to find harmony with Him through His Son, who lived a virtuous life and died to correct the world's social and personal ills. Jesus' ethic perfects society and provides for eternity.

Yin and Yang

The second great Chinese religion is Taoism. A mysterious figure named Lao-tzu, who may be more legend than real, is credited with starting Taoism at the same time Confucianism began. It takes its name from the "Tao," meaning "the way," a basic essence underlying the universe. Even in the West, the Taoist circle of curled black and white halves representing the opposites of yin and yang within the universe appears everywhere.

If Lao-tzu existed at all, he was born about 600 BC. He taught a few disciples while serving as keeper of records for a public official. But he grew embittered at government and resigned to pursue a simple, passive life. He thought that imposing outer laws on people displays the failure of inner morals, leading to rebellion and disrupting nature's harmony. Far better to allow the Tao to take its natural course.

Lao-tzu wanted out of government service, but when he tried to escape the province, the border guard stopped him until he wrote down his ideas. The resulting booklet, the *Tao te Ching*, became the basis of Taoism. Not all

Chinese scholars believe the book was written by a real Lao-tzu, or even that it came from the sixth century BC. But whenever it was written, it advises minimal government, telling rulers how to lead by passive nonaction.

A second leading Taoist figure, Chuang-tzu, wrote over thirty books in the fourth century BC. He expanded the thoughts found in the *Tao te Ching,* although some believe he wrote it. He believed one could take a more active stance in self-transformation, a more intentional realignment with the Tao through self-realization.

Taoism includes a philosophy and a religion. The first emerged about 300 BC and sees the Tao as the final reality toward which we move if freed from outer restraints. Religious Taoism arose about AD 200 when the emperor built a temple to honor Lao-tzu. The trappings of religion soon followed, including sacred writings and a priesthood. Mystical techniques are employed to channel the Tao's forces and gain immortality.

The Tao can't really be known or even named. It might be thought of as the balance of opposites, yin and yang, which include positive and negative, male and female, good and evil, light and dark. To know the Tao, to the degree we can, is to believe that all opposites blend together. When we passively accept them we live in harmony with nature.

Taoists may dismiss the use of reason when weighing religious ideas. They say that truth lies in the contradiction, not the resolution of conflicting thoughts. Christians find common ground when they ponder similar questions such as the nature of reality and the meaning of life.

But Taoism fails to give us a satisfactory guide. No ethic can be found by merging good and evil into one, and no hope is offered by denying the reality of the self. But if a personal God exists, hope and ethics can be found and followed. And Taoists should be attracted to Jesus passively accepting His harsh treatment during His arrest, trials, and crucifixion. Through that door, we can explain His mercy and why He died for us, Christian and Taoist alike.

Thoroughly Japanese

The Pacific theater of World War II witnessed a secret weapon from Japan—kamikaze, "the divine wind." Heavily armed aircraft with only enough fuel to reach their target deliberately flew into enemy ships, creating enormous damage and bringing certain suicide to the pilots. This fanatical devotion strikes Westerners as strange but becomes more understandable against the backdrop of Shinto, the traditional Japanese national religion.

This historic faith traces its origin to early mythology. According to folklore, a male and female god created the world, giving special attention to the islands of Japan. These gods' sexual union produced nature and the lesser gods called *kami,* including the sun goddess *Amaterasu.* The Japanese descended from the *kami,* their Emperor directly from *Amaterasu.*

These ancestral views were first called "Shinto" in the sixth century AD to distinguish them from Buddhism, a new arrival from China. Two hundred years later, professional priests recorded the mythology in two sacred writings—the *Kojiki*, "the record of ancient matters," and the *Nihongi*, "the chronicles of Japan."

After a period of religious conflict, a Buddhist became emperor, and ideas from Buddhism, Confucianism, and Taoism were allowed to merge with Shinto. But by the eighteenth century, a Shinto resurgence occurred as the classical texts were studied with renewed enthusiasm. The people discovered that their country was created by the gods and they descended from the gods. Therefore, they and their nation were superior to all others, a belief that led to Japan's intense nationalism and suicidal resolve prior to and during World War II.

Shinto believes that if we purify ourselves from the world's pollutants like blood or disease, the *kami* protect us. Therefore, one must perform a ritual cleansing before entering a Shinto shrine. The most sacred place in the shrine, the *shintai,* contains a holy object, perhaps a sword, in which lives a *kami* spirit who receives the devotee's worship. Like other Eastern religions, Shinto holds to reincarnation. Many homes include altars where ancestors are venerated because they believe the departed soul might even live near the family.

Shinto is less a set of theological ideas than a cultural mindset. So they rarely express their religion in an organized system as Christians do. A worthy life comes from a pure soul more than compliance with precise beliefs. In contrast to Western individualism, group loyalty and duty (rather than doctrine) are the highest values, as demonstrated by the kamikaze pilots.

Since they think they descended from the gods, few Japanese believe they need a savior. Furthermore, because of their intense group loyalty, Shinto believers may interpret individual decisions for Christ as threats to the community. Therefore, Christians are wise to stress group images like the family of God and the body of Christ. The Shinto need for purity to approach the gods provides a starting point for discussion. Our impurity, sin, alienates us from God and keeps us out of His family. But His perfect Son paid the price to purify us, allowing us to become His eternal child.

Spirits Everywhere

Tens of millions of people worldwide are animists, believing that nature is full of spirits who influence their lives. Animism is thus polytheistic, believing in many "gods" who inhabit animals, plants, and objects. These traditional religions vary from Arctic peoples in northern Siberia to the tribes of Africa. In some places their ideas have merged with more structured religions like Hinduism, Buddhism, and even Roman Catholicism.

Animist religions are not grounded in written Scripture but in oral tradition. Beliefs and practices are usually memorized and passed on by word of mouth. Written records of rituals and stories may exist, but these don't form a "divine word" as in more organized religions.

Most animists believe in one supreme spirit, the Great Spirit or Sky God. This God may be personal or impersonal but is distant from humans. The spirit world between that God and us includes personal beings as well as impersonal spiritual energy. Some of those spirits are deceased ancestors. Others are nature spirits who possess power over part of nature but are tied to one place and depend on our sacrifices. Since they can do us harm or good, animists live in fear of offending them, and practice divination to appease them. If we placate the spirits they'll treat us well and may intercede for us to the supreme God.

Experts on rituals and magic who function as healers and mediums may be called shamans, medicine men, witch doctors, or priests. They honor or pacify the spirits and departed ancestors or try to harness their power to help us in the physical world.

Traditional African religions vary from tribe to tribe, but most of them south of the Sahara are animist. Africans are much more communal than Westerners, thus their religions are determined more by the tribe or group than by personal belief. But, as in other types of animism, people focus more on the spirits than on the supreme God in daily life.

Native-American religions are also hard to summarize because they vary greatly among different tribes, but they too are animistic. Perhaps more than others, Native Americans may associate the supreme God with something they see, such as the sun or an animal. Their totem poles are not idols as such, but they carry spiritual significance or record ancestral history and tribal legends.

As modernization infringes on traditional cultures, animist religions become less visible, but they're not necessarily vanishing. They tend to incorporate elements of organized religion and modern society without rejecting their own heritage. Traditional peoples may follow their practices in secret without abandoning them.

Christians have more in common with animists than they might first think. Their beliefs should remind modern Christians that the spirit world is real. We dare not become closet naturalists while claiming to believe in the spiritual realm. Christians and animists both believe that life's deepest problems result from offending Someone in that spirit world, and the solution must come from there as well. That similar view provides opportunity for sharing the good news of Christ who once and for all satisfied the Supreme God who is offended by our sin. Therefore, we need not fear retaliation from the spirits. The Supreme God will protect all who come to Him through His Son.

Can God's Prophet Err?

Most of us have answered the knock on the door to find a pair of Jehovah's Witnesses eager to do battle over the deity of Christ. The Jehovah's Witnesses are one of the world's most successful new religions with twelve million active and inactive members. The Watchtower Society claims to be God's sole source of revelation and understanding on earth: "Jehovah's organization alone, in all the earth, is directed by God's holy spirit or active force. . . . To it alone God's Sacred Word, the Bible, is not a sealed book."[39] They further allege that they are Jehovah's prophet: "This 'prophet' was not one man but was a body of men and women. . . . Today they are known as Jehovah's Christian Witnesses."[40]

They were founded in 1879 by Charles Taze Russell when he split from William Miller, founder of the Adventist movement. For the next thirty-five years, Russell led the Witnesses despite his lack of theological training. During that time he wrote the seven-volume *Studies in the Scriptures*, which he asserted came through divine inspiration. Though largely neglected

89

NEW RELIGIONS

today, these writings were the early source of the Witnesses' theology that continues today.

Unfortunately, the Witnesses have experienced repeated prophetic failure. For decades, they predicted that the Battle of Armageddon would be fought in 1914, followed by the end of the world. When 1914 passed without Armageddon or the end, they recalculated their figures, resulting in future prophetic failures. Observers are right to wonder about repeated errors from a group that presumes to be God's one, true prophet. Something seems amiss.

Throughout their history, the Witnesses have alleged a level of scholarship in the biblical languages that matches their lofty claim as God's sole prophetic voice. But in 1954 this claim to scholarship was publicly exposed as a fraud. Jehovah's Witness President Frederick Franz was considered their most learned Hebrew scholar. But under oath in a court of law, he proved incapable of handling even the most basic Hebrew.

The Witnesses' main deviation from Christianity is their view of the Trinity. They believe that Jesus was created by God, and thus not God Himself. They also deny the reality of the Holy Spirit, believing this refers not to a person but only to the impersonal force of Jehovah acting in the world. And they teach salvation by works, believing that Jesus' death did not accomplish everything needed to save us. It merely gives us a second chance to earn salvation by performing the proper works.

To support their doctrines, they cite legitimate Bible translations when they can. But since the Bible does not generally endorse their views, they published their own translation in 1961, *The New World Translation* (NWT). As the product of their own people, none of whom are recognized as Greek or Hebrew scholars, it's full of predictable errors and obvious bias. Genuine scholars consider it seriously flawed, even dishonest—a mere tool for propagating their nonbiblical teachings. Dr. Julius Mantey, one of the world's leading Greek scholars, said of the NWT, "I have never read any New Testament so badly translated. . . . It is a distortion of the New Testament."[41] Witnesses' apparent fear of reading any material but their own makes them a hard group to reach. But, by using a King James Version or a 1901 American Standard Bible, we can challenge their interpretation of key verses in light of the larger context. Jehovah's Witnesses recognize those two translations, even though neither includes the Witnesses' peculiar interpretations. We can demonstrate even from their own translation that salvation is received by faith (Titus 3:5; Ephesians

2:8-9), that Christ is God (John 5:18; John 20:28), and that the Holy Spirit is God (Acts 5:3).

The most important preparation the Christian needs to engage a Witness is thorough study of Scripture. Biblical truth is the spiritual ammunition the Spirit uses in our conversations with groups that deviate from His Word. Daily immersion in His Word prepares us for the inevitable knock on the door.

Joseph's Kids

Slick TV and newspaper ads sell the Church of Jesus Christ of Latter Day Saints (LDS) as a Christian denomination. But is it? Are Mormons just another flavor of historic Christianity like Presbyterians, Lutherans, or Baptists?

The Mormon Church claims to be the world's fastest growing religion. Estimates put their global membership at ten million and their full-time missionary roles at 65,000. Their explosive growth rate is matched by their vast wealth. Consistent tithing and industrious work habits have reaped a multi-billion dollar operation with vast holdings in real estate, insurance, broadcasting, utilities, and agriculture.

Joseph Smith spent his early life dabbling with the occult and digging for treasure. At fourteen, he allegedly received a visit from God the Father and Jesus Christ telling him to restore "true Christianity." He claimed a second vision at age seventeen, this one from an angel named Nephi, later changed to Moroni. Moroni's visit

90

NEW RELIGIONS

was the first of several over the next four years, during which he told the young treasure hunter where to find some golden plates and the "Urim and Thummim," referring to two items worn in the breastplate of the Jewish High Priest (Exodus 28:13-30). They were thought by some scholars to be associated with receiving the Lord's guidance. Smith adopted the phrase to suggest that they would help him understand the writing on the plates. Smith then translated those "Reformed Egyptian" writings (as he called them) into what became the *Book of Mormon*, and soon founded his new church.

Along with the *Book of Mormon*, their scriptures include *Doctrine and Covenants* and *The Pearl of Great Price*. The Bible is accepted, but only as far as it's translated correctly, that is, according to Mormon doctrine.

Some of the obvious Mormon deviations from Christianity, in their own words, are as follows:

1. Many gods have always existed. In the words of Brigham Young: "How many gods are there? I do not know. But there never was a time when there were not gods."[42]

2. God is an evolved human and humans can evolve into gods: "As man is, God once was: as God is, man may become."[43]

3. God the Father has a physical body: "The

Father has a body of flesh and bones as tangible as man's. . . . "[44]

4. God the Father reproduces spirit children with His female counterpart: "Implicit in the Christian verity that all men are the spirit children of an *Eternal Father* is the usually unspoken truth that they are also the offspring of an *Eternal Mother*. An exalted and glorified Man of Holiness could not be a Father unless a Woman of like glory, perfection, and holiness was associated with him as a mother."[45]

5. Jesus was born of the sexual union between God the Father and Mary: "His [Christ's] unique status in the flesh as the offspring of a mortal mother [Mary] and of an immortal, or resurrected and glorified Father [Elohim]."[46]

6. Jesus was a polygamist who reproduced children through His own multiple marriages: ". . . Jesus Christ was married at Cana of Galilee, that Mary, Martha, and others were his wives, and that he begat children."[47]

7. Jesus is not the second Person of the Trinity as understood by Christians, but a lesser god and Satan's brother: "But both the Scriptures and the prophets affirm that Jesus Christ and Lucifer are indeed offspring of our Heaven Father and, therefore, spirit brothers. . . . Jesus was Lucifer's older brother."[48]

Humans preexist their physical birth and are the same species as God. Mankind's fall in the Garden of Eden, which was located near modern Independence, Missouri, was deliberate and good because it enabled us to make further spiritual progress. Christ's death ensures the redemption of all mankind, although in different levels of heaven. His atonement, however, did not remove our personal sins. It merely gives us the chance to do so by our own good works. Salvation is thus earned by our obedience.

Mormonism suffers from several major shortcomings. Joseph Smith changed the story of his visions several times. The *Book of Mormon* and *Doctrines and Covenants* have been changed thousands of times, yet they still contradict one another. Mormon prophecies, including those of Joseph Smith, did not come true. Modern archaeology and textual studies refute the writing and claims of Mormon books.

Christians should beware that Mormons use Christian terms but give them different meanings. Therefore, asking for and giving precise definitions is a must for meaningful conversation. Whatever we might think of Mormonism, we should not mistake it for Christianity.

Neither Grapes nor Nuts

The Christian Science Monitor has for years been known and respected for objective coverage of the news. Despite the obvious name, not everyone remembers that it's the newspaper of Christian Science, a religion whose authority still resides in its long dead founder, Mary Baker Eddy (1821-1910). Eddy believed that Christianity had lost its healing component and she was returning to its roots. Christian Science seeks to lead people to God as the means of good health through psychic healing. But in recent decades this once-fashionable group has been declining, with current membership estimated at only about 200,000.

Eddy suffered from poor health much of her life, and in 1862, she began receiving treatments from Phineas P. Quimby, who claimed to heal without medicine by a method he called "the Science of Christ." In 1866, she said she nearly died from injuries suffered in a fall, injuries that Dr. Alvin Cushing, her attending physician, denied were serious. But within a week she announced that she was healed by reading Matthew 9:2, which tells

91

NEW RELIGIONS

of Jesus healing a paralyzed man.

In 1875, she published *Science and Health with Key to the Scriptures*, which she said she received through divine revelation, although it plagiarizes huge amounts of material from Quimby and a dissertation by Dr. Francis Lieber.[49] She soon began her own healing ministry, also teaching it to others for a fee of $300, a sizeable sum at the time. In 1879, she incorporated the Church of Christ, Scientist, changed to The First Church of Christ Scientist in 1892.

After several decades of selling itself as a Christian denomination without "offensive" Christian doctrines like hell, the Trinity, or the blood of Christ, Christian Science has fallen on hard times. In the last generation, it has suffered from declining membership, bad press, and financial struggles. But, as with all counterfeit religions, resurgence is hoped for by the faithful.

Like most newly designed religions, Christian Science gives lip service to the Bible. The real authority, however, is Mary Baker Eddy's writings, especially *Science and Health with Key to the Scriptures*, as interpreted by the Christian Science Church Board of Directors. She claimed that her teachings came from the Bible, but her allegorical methods of interpreting it made it say whatever she wanted it to say. She alleged to have received the final revelation of truth.[50]

Christian Science differs across the board from historic Christianity. It portrays God as a pantheistic, divine principle, not an infinite, personal Spirit. Jesus was not God, nor did He return from the dead because He never really died. The Christ is the manifestation of God, and the Holy Spirit is Christian Science. Scripture includes errors. Man is not material but spiritual and part of God. Sin, death, and a physical universe do not exist. Since there is no sin, salvation is unneeded, although salvation is sometimes presented as becoming aware of the unreality of the material realm. Healing is real and the expression of "primitive" Christianity.

Like the cereal Grape-Nuts, which is neither grapes nor nuts, Christian Science is neither Christian nor science. It has nothing in common with Christianity, renouncing every major Christian doctrine, or science, which it rejects just as easily. This religious movement may be on the decline, but it still poses a threat to the spiritually unwary.

New but Old

Tens of millions of Americans dabble with New Age techniques or ideas. The New Age Movement (NAM) permeates the media and influences schools, business, and government. It is not a single cult or religion, although its ideas ride the coattails of many cults and religions. This collection of unconnected movements shares common beliefs but no central organization. It offers a new worldview—a different way of seeing truth and reality. It represents the replacement of Western atheistic materialism with Eastern pantheistic mysticism.

The NAM is not new. "New Age" ideas can be found in the occultism of the great ancient empires. It survived the centuries in various mystery religions and resurfaced in more structured form in the Theosophical Society of the nineteenth century. Merging with elements of Darwinian evolutionary theory, it provided an alternative to the hopelessness of materialism that was replacing Christianity in the West. Ideas of a "collective consciousness" from psychologist Carl Jung were thrown into the mix in the early twentieth century.

The 1960s counterculture set the stage for a massive resurgence of New Age ideas, especially among young people. In the sixties and seventies, an infusion of Asian immigrants brought Eastern beliefs into a culture that was increasingly open to "new" ideas. In time the hippie generation traded flower power for paying jobs, but didn't abandon their New Age beliefs. The establishment that received this new generation of leaders and workers also inherited their pantheistic mysticism. The eighties and nineties saw an explosion of books, movies, and seminars openly pushing New Ageism. As a result of being championed by Hollywood celebrities, it is now mainstream.

The NAM does not have one Scripture or authority. It believes that special revelation continues and is progressive. The teaching of today's gurus scuttles what Jesus and other "Ascended Masters" taught in the past. When New Age proponents can make the Bible support their views, they claim to believe it. When it doesn't, which is most of the time, they reject it.

Classifying New Age beliefs is not easy. Diverse groups inevitably disagree on details. But the following themes appear among most committed New Agers: God is pantheistic, an impersonal consciousness. All is one, and nature is an illusion. Jesus was not "the Christ" but an enlightened teacher. Life is cyclical including reincarnation. Spirit beings reveal "truth" to us. Humans are God, evolving into deity as we become aware of our true identity. We help this process by expanding our consciousness with Eastern meditation and occult techniques. No final truth exists; all is relative.

Talking with New Agers is not easy because of their diverse views. Christians might approach a topic from one angle, only to discover that our conversation partner doesn't hold that view. So, we should explore the other person's beliefs before we offer our position. We must also define our terms since they may use Christian words but don't mean what we do.

The church needs to return to serious, systematic teaching of the Bible, theology, apologetics, and church history. Without consistent training in the truth, Christians will remain unprepared for spiritual battle and may not recognize the subtle distortions presented by New Age ideas. Nice little devotionals to make people feel good will not carry the day on the field of spiritual combat.

Watching the Moon

Airports and shopping centers of the 1970s and 1980s were filled with smiling young people selling flowers and candy. These eager entrepreneurs raised funds for various causes that tugged the heartstrings and wallets of an unsuspecting public. Their social programs and conservative values drew the approval of politicians and religious leaders. But most of the money went to the Unification Church, known as the Moonies.

Yong Myung Moon was born in 1920 in what is now North Korea. Even though his Confucian family converted to Presbyterianism when he was ten, he continued to contact his spirit ancestors for years. He claims a vision from Jesus sometime between age fifteen and eighteen—the reports vary. Christ told Moon to complete the task that He (Christ) failed to do. In the mid-1940s, Moon founded a monastery and organized his teaching into what was later called the *Divine Principle*. He changed his name to Sun Myung Moon, established the Unification Church in 1954, and published his

Divine Principle three years later.

Between 1972 and 1974 Moon toured America, calling people to abandon their churches and prepare for the second coming of Christ. The Kingdom of Heaven was to arrive on earth in the year 1981. Despite his alleged visits to the spirit world to consult with Buddha, Jesus, and God the Father, he missed his 1981 prediction. Most of his followers believed he referred to himself when he spoke of the "Lord of the Second Advent," and he announced in 1992 that he was the Messiah.

Because Moonies consider the Bible unreliable and largely misunderstood, it is believed that God gave the correct interpretation to Moon. His higher revelations include truth for the current age that had not been given before. He uses Christian terms but alters the content, basing much of his doctrine on Taoist yin and yang dualism. Even God is dualistic, the Holy Spirit being the female part of God's nature.

The Fall occurred when Eve committed adultery with Satan then had sexual intercourse with Adam, thus contaminating the human race. Jesus was supposed to remedy this mess by marrying a bride—another Eve—and reproducing sinless children. The Crucifixion was an unplanned mistake, which saved us spiritually but not physically. Another Messiah was needed to complete Jesus' failed work by marrying the perfect bride and producing sinless children. Moon and his wife are this new Adam and Eve, the "True Parents" of the human race. Through matched marriages blessed by Moon, sinless children are born, thus salvation spreads.

Moon's fund-raising efforts and business enterprises have generated vast sums of money. It is well-documented that he justifies deception and outright lies in solicitations by saying it's done for good.[51] His complex business empire controls hundreds of companies worldwide worth tens of billions of dollars. Many of them are disguised under other names to avoid scrutiny, but in 1982 he was convicted of income tax evasion and spent eighteen months in prison.

When talking with a Moonie, be ready for courteous deception, as Moon has directed. But, we might ask, if Moon deceives and manipulates, how do Moonies know he hasn't deceived them? Thousands of former members have testified that Moon is untrustworthy. Only the true Jesus dealt honestly with everyone, and He offers the eternal fulfillment Moon cannot. Moon is not the Messiah, nor is his Unification Church true Christianity.

Passive No Longer

Most Christians show little concern over Unitarian Universalism (UU). For the past generation its declining numbers and passive stance toward others made it seem nonthreatening. But UU is no longer content to ride in the back of the religious bus. After recharging its batteries, it sells itself more aggressively than it used to. And its influence is bigger than its numbers—it claims more entries, proportionately, in *Who's Who* than does any other religious body.

The modern Unitarian Universalist Association began in 1961 as a merger of two distinct groups, Universalists and Unitarians. The core belief of the first was that everyone would be saved and go to heaven. That group first organized in 1793. The second group was formed in 1825 to emphasize the unity of God rather than a Trinity.

Unitarianism evolved from sixteenth-century heretics and nonconformists. They opposed the Trinity and Christ's deity, but, strangely, thought they were Christ's true followers. The seventeenth-century "Father of English Unitarianism," John Biddle, wrote against the Trinity, but believed he did so from within Christianity, even using Scripture to support his views. William Channing advanced Unitarianism in America before Ralph Waldo Emerson moved it from a quasi-Christian context into a fully man-centered philosophy complete with pantheistic overtones.

Traditional Universalism has also changed. It reinterpreted its own view of universal *salvation* to mean a universal *religion*, combining elements of many faiths. Today the humanist foundation of UU is shrinking as it adds New Age mysticism to its ideas.

The cornerstone of UU is not a set of beliefs, but freethinking humanism. They consider the Bible, including its "errors," merely a history of Israel's religious evolution. Therefore, it offers nothing more than inspiration. Authority and truth are not found in supernatural revelation, but in whatever the individual chooses to believe. Consequently, UU holds no official statement of faith, each person owning her own set of convictions. But the following beliefs are common: God is not a Trinity and may not exist at all. If "He" does, it's some form of impersonal pantheism. Jesus was a good man, maybe a great moral teacher, but not Deity. Mankind is the highest result of evolution thus far, but the process continues.

We are essentially good and therefore need no Savior. By our own moral improvement we achieve whatever "salvation" we may think we want.

UU is a more serious threat to Christianity than it was in the past, in part because it's grown more hostile to Christianity. But a beachhead for discussion exists. Its members claim to be rational, tolerant seekers of truth. Reality may prove otherwise, but their boast of openness can be used as a wedge to begin discussion about Christ. Refusal to talk about the plausibility of Christianity leaves them open to the accusation of bias—a charge they cannot stomach. If they resist such dialogue, reasonable people might wonder if they are as narrow as those they accuse of bigotry. One might think that a true seeker would honestly explore the claims of Christ and the evidence behind them.

Dreams Fulfilled

Many Christians adhere to the "prosperity gospel"—a belief that God always intends His children to be happy, healthy, and wealthy. If we experience sickness or poverty, we either don't know God, or lack faith, or have sin in our lives. This view germinated over a century ago in "The Unity School of Christianity." Their hook was selling the hope of dreams fulfilled. But is "Unity" Christian or something else?

Unity's formal membership is only about 100,000, but its influence surpasses its numbers. Through radio and mailings it offers hundreds of books and tapes, sends out millions of publications each year, and receives millions of prayer requests. Those who follow the "positive thinking" path to life are, perhaps unknowingly, using "Unity" ideas. And some aspects of the modern charismatic movement originated with Unity. Most people who contact the group believe they're receiving help from Christians as their name suggests.

Unity's founder, Charles Fillmore, was born on a reservation in 1854, and was initiated into the Indians' mystical ceremonies as a boy. In 1881, he married Myrtle, who had suffered from tuberculosis much of her life. After contracting malaria a few years later, she was given only six months to live. But she was healed as a result of what she learned and used from a spiritist group called New Thought. Charles was skeptical, so he explored Christian Science, Eastern religions, and various forms of spiritism in search of answers. He applied the meditation techniques he learned from his study, and his own withered leg was allegedly healed. Based on those experiences, the Fillmores founded a new religion, eventually known as the Unity School of Christianity.

Unity claims respect for all the Scriptures of the world, but, they say, truth is more than a text. Revelation conveys experience as well as information—a classic belief of nearly all forms of mysticism. If one has a weak relationship with God, he might find help in the Bible if interpreted from Unity's perspective, which means Charles Fillmore's views.

Unity downplays the importance of belief systems, rating theology below the pursuit of health, happiness, and prosperity. As with most mind sciences, they use Christian terms but redefine them to their own liking. Similar to other forms of pantheism, God is an impersonal, infinite mind. Our consciousness and God's are one. Jesus was not God but a man who reached awareness of His inner divine self. The Cross and Resurrection are examples of mind over matter. Since the Fall is false thinking, we can renew ourselves through right thinking. If we think positively enough, we shouldn't lack anything we want or encounter anything bad.

Unity uses "Christianity" in its name, but it's not Christian at all. Few of Unity's followers know the Bible or Christian history. As with many modern religions, they simply believe what their leaders tell them is true. And Fillmore taught that today's Christian doctrine did not originate 2,000 years ago, but was invented a mere 300 years ago. That, of course, is not true, as a quick survey of church history reveals. Fillmore also claimed that he wouldn't die, but he did. So did Jesus. But after He claimed to be one with the Father, He returned from the grave to prove what He said. Charles Fillmore did not. Christians should beware of his nonChristian "religion" that uses the Christian name.

Science Fiction

The wild ideas of Scientology could only come from a science fiction writer, and in fact they did. L. Ron Hubbard was a successful science fiction writer in the 1930s and 1940s. But he tipped his hand in 1949 by declaring that one could make more money creating his own religion. Right on cue, a year later he published *Dianetics: A Modern Science of Mental Health*. In 1950, after seeing the huge success of *Dianetics*, he released his first book on Scientology, and the Church of Scientology (CS) was incorporated in 1954.

CS claims to merge ancient Buddhism and modern technology. In truth, it's an outgrowth of Dianetics, the pretended scientific enterprise that eliminates the problems from past lives. It incorporates elements from Eastern religions, pseudo-psychology, and the occult, claiming to free the soul from bondage to matter, thus restoring its pure spiritual condition.

According to a well-respected source on new religious movements, Hubbard's personal history is checkered with lies, multiple marriages, and occult connections—

hardly the pattern one seeks in a religious leader.[52] And his CS has kept pace with him by getting into repeated legal scrapes with individuals and governments.[53]

The Church developed a reputation for harassing and pressuring ex-members and critics. Even the U.S. government was the target of a three-year spy operation that included over 5,000 Scientology agents. The CS sued the FDA over the legitimacy of the "e-meter," that Scientology says is medical equipment, and the IRS over giving religious organization status to Scientology.

Authority within CS lies solely with Hubbard whose writings are recognized as "Scripture." He claims that Scientology does not contradict other religions because the truth he reveals originated in their ancient writings. The Bible is largely neglected because it's only a modern spin-off of Hindu Scripture.

Scientology's beliefs are creative and complex. Only a brief sample of definitions can be included here. A "thetan" is comparable to the human soul. An "engram" is a past experience, even from past lives. "Overts" are mistakes. An "e-meter" is a piece of equipment that measures electrical resistance, recording a person's responses to questions, something like a lie-detector. An "audit" is the interview during which the e-meter is used. A person who has dealt with past negative experiences is called "clear." "Operating Thetan" is a phrase used for different levels of spiritual development.

Hubbard's theology retains a crude outline of Eastern beliefs. God or gods might exist. Jesus was not the Savior, but one of several Messiahs, just above the "clear" level. Mankind is basically good, but trapped in the cycle of reincarnation, which began 60 trillion years ago. Scientology frees us and helps us pursue our evolutionary path to become godlike. This enlightenment of the thetan within (salvation) is accomplished, predictably, by erasing our engrams through the rather pricey audit process. That sounds a bit like Eastern belief, except that money rather than ascetic self-discipline is the means of soul liberation.

Scientology teachings have no basis in science, and present a bizarre distortion of what Eastern religions really believe. But we should give Hubbard credit. He was a good science fiction writer who announced his intentions ahead of time, and pulled it off. He made a ton of money creating his own religion.

Which Way Is the Right Way?

The Way is not a church but a multi-million dollar research and study group that offers "true Biblical understanding and Christian living." It sells itself as the original version of Christianity that everyone else has lost.

The Way exists to spread the teaching of its founder, Victor Paul Wierwille (1916-1985). His use of Greek and Hebrew to verify his extreme views sounds impressive to those who don't know otherwise. But his conclusions are not supported by genuine scholars. Wierwille's doctoral degree typifies bogus academic claims. He received it from a place called Pikes Peak Seminary, a degree mill without faculty or accreditation.

The Way began, like many manmade religions, with an encounter between God and a chosen person. Wierwille claims that God audibly spoke to him in 1942, promising that he would teach the Bible like no one since the first century. Wierwille was skeptical, so he asked for a sign—snow. God, of course, came through and made it snow like crazy. Wierwille accepted his divine commission, and The Way now teaches truths from God lost since the time of Paul.

The Way remained small until the late 1960s Jesus movement expanded their numbers. Responding to unexpected growth, they started a more structured leadership and missionary training program. But their growth also increased visibility and scrutiny, raising alarm over psychological and spiritual intimidation, weapons and survival training, and their own police force. When Wierwille died in 1985, The Way splintered into smaller, spin-off groups, although The Way International continues.

They say the Bible is their sole authority. But, they continue, because today's Bible includes errors, we have to rely on Dr. Wierwille's teachings to interpret it properly. Furthermore, only some of the Bible is authoritative for Christians today; the rest of the Bible is relegated to second-class status. While demoting the Bible, Wierwille claimed divine inspiration for some of his own writings, equating them with the words of the Holy Spirit.

The Way recruits on college campuses, showing concern and friendship to lonely young people. Once in the group, life is tightly controlled. The recruiting techniques and regimen of exercise, work, and meetings have been described by former members as manipulative, even brainwashing.[54] Evangelical churches are also recruiting fields for The Way. Unsuspecting Christians are invited to Bible studies without knowing what they're getting into. The hook is the promise of success, health, and happiness. Those with shallow biblical knowledge can fall for this trick.

The Way uses Christian vocabulary and claims to be orthodox, but it holds bizarre doctrines, including the following: It denies the Trinity, viewing it as a pagan idea. God is one person; Jesus is the created Son of God. The capitalized Holy Spirit is a synonym for God; the lower case holy spirit refers to spiritual power. Only seven of Paul's epistles hold value for today's church; the rest of the Bible is neglected. Salvation is received by grace but proven by speaking in tongues, and it guarantees health and wealth. Death is followed by soul sleep not conscious existence, and unbelievers are annihilated rather than eternally punished.

Rejecting or changing major doctrines moves one outside the circle of orthodoxy. Wierwille's teaching violates the Bible at numerous points, as careful study reveals. Despite its claims, The Way is not Christian.

Knock, Knock.
Who's There?

From earliest times man has believed that death does not end our existence. We want our loved ones and ourselves to live on, and we do. Spiritism (sometimes called spiritualism) offers contact with the dead whose spirits remain nearby. It draws people because it presents hope, confirming our longing for eternal existence. Such contacts usually occur during a seance, by means of a medium, a link between the physical and spirit worlds. Even in our age of high technology, estimates of practicing spiritists range from twenty to fifty million worldwide.

The modern resurgence of spiritism began in Hydesville, New York, in 1848. Margaret and Katie Fox, ages fifteen and twelve, said they heard mysterious noises. Concluding that a spirit was the source, they devised a code for communicating—a series of taps for "No" or "Yes" answers. Neighbors witnessed and verified the nightly tapping sessions. The news spread and spiritism grew at a frantic pace. Years later, when the Fox sisters confessed that they had created the tapping by popping their toes, the nationwide fascination dropped like a rock, but didn't die. Spiritism increased after each of the two world wars, and has grown again since the 1960s after Episcopal Bishop James Pike tried to reach his dead son on live TV.

The authority for spiritism is not written revelation but experience. What happens, rather than what's revealed, determines what's true. So, they don't evaluate their experience by the Bible, but interpret the Bible by their experience. They even say the Bible endorses spiritism, and Jesus was a medium.

Spiritism holds no formal set of beliefs, but it affirms some core principles. Spiritists accept an Infinite Intelligence. Humans continue after death, and people here can talk to those departed spirits. Morality is found in the Golden Rule, and we are responsible for how we live. After death we receive our reward for this life as we follow the path of endless progression in reincarnation. Jesus was one of many Saviors who came to enlighten us. He is divine only in the sense that we are all divine. His resurrection is rejected, and salvation is unneeded because there was never a Fall and there is no sin.

What happens during those alleged encounters with

the dead? Let's consider the possibilities: (1) Perhaps they're what spiritists claim—contact with the dead. But facts revealed by these "spirits" are often wrong, and former mediums admit that it's not real. (2) At least a few are faked because some mediums are exposed as frauds. (3) Scientists suggest a natural explanation beyond our current knowledge—perhaps an unexplored realm of ESP. A few of these weird events might fall into this area. (4) The Bible acknowledges the spiritual dimension inhabited by evil spirits. But despite the Bible's warning not to dabble in that unseen world (Leviticus 19:31), some people do, and may reach demons who sell themselves as dear departed brother Ned.

Trying to contact the dead violates the Bible and leads to serious danger. And because Christians have access to God through Christ, we don't need to pursue other sources of comfort or guidance. We are wise to heed the Bible's command to test the spirits (1 John 4:1). Spiritism rejects every major Christian doctrine. It is at best fraudulent, and at worst demonic.

I'm Out of Here

Eckankar is a New Age belief system that claims to be the oldest religion in the world—the ancient science of soul travel. It teaches people how to find spiritual freedom by looking within to expand their consciousness. By practicing spiritual exercises, they come in contact with the light and sound of God. Eckankar blends mystical experience with occult philosophy but sells itself to the unsuspecting by downplaying its more bizarre elements. Therefore, unlike some religious groups that have caught the public eye, such as Scientology, Eckankar keeps a low profile, avoiding intense scrutiny. Many people have never even heard of it.

Eckankar was created in 1965 by Paul Twitchell, a dabbler in Eastern religions who announced that he was the 971st Eck Master, an incarnation of God. (Eckists don't believe their religion was founded then, but only resurfaced after being forgotten for centuries.) But instead of being the original, one true religion, Eckankar is a modified collection of ideas from Hindu teacher

66 | NEW RELIGIONS

Kirpal Singh. Twitchell had been part of Singh's group in the fifties.

His theft of ideas is also evident in his book *The Tiger's Fang.* He copied whole sections from the writings of Dr. Julian Johnson, who promoted Eastern beliefs in the West. After Twitchell died in 1971, Darwin Gross took command of Eckankar for the next decade as the 972nd Eck Master. Eckankar is now headquartered in Chanhassen, Minnesota, under the leadership of Harold Klemp, the current Eck Master.[55]

This group believes that Christianity has changed from its beginnings. The Bible is now full of mistakes but still contains hidden teachings that promote soul travel. Eckankar does claim a Scripture of its own, called the Shariyat-Ki-Sugmad. The original is in a spiritual city known as Agam Des, which can be visited only by astral projection, soul travel. In the meantime, Eckists receive guidance from the living Eck Master through dreams and spiritual exercises as well as his writings. Thus, like all human-based religions, authority lies in the person at the top of the spiritual food chain.

Eckankar's beliefs retain the residue of their Eastern heritage. God is an impersonal, pantheistic spirit that can be known as light and sound. We contact the light and sound of God through spiritual exercises. Jesus was a great religious teacher but, like Buddha, Lao-tzu, and others, was a follower of Eck. Each of us is the Truth itself, divine sparks that "fell" into the material world and now suffer spiritual ignorance. We attain salvation by the enlightenment received through soul travel resulting from our spiritual exercises. As we participate in the sound of God during such experiences, we're freed from the cycle of reincarnation.

Eckankar is a clever creation of an inventive mind. Unlike most New Age religions, which believe many paths lead to God or truth or enlightenment, Eckankar claims to be the only way.

Whose Family?

Much of what we know about the secretive group called The Family comes from Deborah Davis' book, *The Children of God* (Zondervan, 1984). She is the eldest daughter of David "Moses" Berg, the group's founder. After leaving the sect, she became a Christian and exposed the inner workings of her father's "family."

In the late 1960s, Berg ran a Christian coffee house in California. But plagued by what he called "persecution," he and about fifty followers fled.[56] He left his wife, whom he called "the old church," to live with one of his disciples, predictably identified as "the new church." While they wandered across the country, one reporter called them the Children of God, and the name stuck.

The main group landed in Texas and began colonizing new communities nationwide. About this time, Berg announced that God had sent a 700-year-old spirit named Abrahim as his guide. When "persecution" arose again, they went underground and scattered to other countries. During the 1990s, The Children of God returned to America as The Family. They've admitted past mistakes in an effort to clean up their image. But they now target liberal churches, searching for converts in this more tolerant mission field.

They originally said that the Bible, King James Version only, was their sole authority. But like many newly devised religions, the only approved interpretation was their leader's, God's prophet for this age. Berg claims to receive divine revelations that he passes to his children through his "Mo Letters." When differences arise between his Letters and the Bible, the latter is rejected, superseded by Berg's new revelation.

The following contradictory teachings appear in his writings and elsewhere within The Family: God is more or less pantheistic but also a sexually active Being. Jesus was created by God or the result of a sexual union between the angel Gabriel and Mary. Jesus fornicated with his female disciples, and now holds orgies in heaven. The Holy Spirit is God's sexy wife with whom Berg had a fling. Since salvation is by grace, we can do whatever we want as long as it's done in love. Everyone will eventually be saved because a second chance to believe will be offered after death. Those who believe in this life will enjoy sexual orgies in "Space City," a pyramid now hidden inside the moon.

Considering the sexual theme that permeates The

Family's "theology," their rampant immorality is not surprising. In the past they even used sex to entice people to join the group—"Flirty Fishing" was the catchy title. God was sharing His wife, the church, with the world to show His love. According to ex-members, various kinds of sexual impropriety were practiced and promoted before the mid-1980s.[57]

Berg died in 1994. His Family now reports only a few thousand members spread across several countries, but experts claim there are many more. They have worked on a new, more respectable image and have joined an organization to defend the rights of new religious groups against counter-cult ministries. They may be a family of sorts, but their legal rights don't make them Children of God by any biblical definition.

Epilogue

So what? Why have we explored all this information about different topics and issues? What's the point? Christianity is true—that's the point! It's not just one option, even the preferred option, among many. It is true. Jesus Christ is who He said He was—the promised Messiah, the Son of God, the Savior of the world.

By thinking honestly, we can investigate the evidence and conclude that the Bible is true. It has and does survive the challenges of critics through the ages. It records accurate facts about the infinite, personal God's deliberate, passionate intervention into the world to save mankind at great cost to Himself.

Other worldviews collapse under scrutiny. Jesus invites us to investigate Him and His claims, to look as deeply and critically as we can, searching under every historical rock and between all the logical lines. When we do, He still stands and lives. His Resurrection is the bedrock of Christianity. There is only one issue—either Jesus is who He said He was and He returned from the dead to prove it, or He is not and did not.

Science is a marvelous tool to explore the wonders of a world created by God and for His glory. We should pursue it with vigor. But God is the Master not the slave of His universe. Thus He can and does intervene, and not always according to the laws He designed. He retains the right to bypass them through what we call miracles.

Some of the world's religions contain points of truth here and there. But they mistake the part for the whole and often distort the rest. They often lead people into serious, even dangerous, errors. But Christians can learn lessons from other religions, not the least of which is that we can do better at presenting our argument for Christianity. We can be more committed, more rational, and more gracious.

I urge the reader to pursue apologetics further. Many wonderful sources are available to explore beyond this introductory book. Some of them are listed in appendix B of this work. All followers of Jesus should remember that the purpose of study is not to accumulate facts or argue a case, but to know the living, risen Christ. He is not the culmination of a debate, but our living, loving Savior.

Through the ages, Jesus' words still place a claim on each life that cannot be casually dismissed. "I am the way and the truth and the life. No one comes to the Father except through me" (John 14:6). "If the Son sets you free, you will be free indeed" (John 8:36). "He who has the Son has life; he who does not have the Son of God does not have life" (1 John 5:12). "I have come that they may have life, and have it to the full" (John 10:10).

Index of Topics

Recommended Books

Ankenberg, J. & J. Weldon, *Encyclopedia of Cults and New Religions*. Eugene, Ore.: Harvest House, 1999.

Beckwith, F. and Gregory K. *Relativism: Feet Firmly Planted in Mid-Air*. Grand Rapids, Mich.: Baker, 1998.

Behe, M. J. *Darwin's Black Box: The Biochemical Challenge to Evolution*. New York: Simon & Schuster, 1998.

Beverley, J. A. *Christ & Islam: Understanding the Faith of the Muslims*. Joplin: College Press, 1997.

_____. *Understanding Islam*. Nashville: Nelson, 2001.

Bloom, A. *The Closing of the American Mind*. New York: Simon and Schuster, 1987.

Boa, K. D. and R. M. Bowman, Jr. *Faith Has Its Reasons: An Integrative Approach to Defending Christianity*. Colorado Springs, Colo.: NavPress, 2001.

Carson, D. A. *The Gagging of God: Christianity Confronts Pluralism*. Grand Rapids, Mich.: Zondervan, 1996.

Carter, S. L. *The Culture of Disbelief: How American Law and Politics Trivialize Religious Devotion*. New York: Doubleday, 1994.

Chandler, R. *Understanding the New Age*. Dallas, Tex.: Word, 1988.

Christian History Magazine. "Christians & Muslims." Issue 74 (Vol. XX1, No. 2).

Colson, C. *Answers to Your Kids' Questions: An Essential Resource for Parents and Youth Leaders*. Wheaton, Ill.: Tyndale, 2000.

Colson, C. and N. Pearcey, *How Now Shall We Live?* Wheaton, Ill.: Tyndale, 1999.

Copan, P. *That's Just Your Interpretation: Responding to Skeptics Who Challenge Your Faith*. Grand Rapids, Mich.: Baker, 2001.

_____. *True for You, But Not for Me*. Minneapolis: Bethany, 1998.

Corduan, W. *Neighboring Faiths: A Christian Introduction to World Religions*. Downers Grove, Ill.: InterVarsity, 1998.

_____. *Reasonable Faith: Basic Christian Apologetics*. Nashville, Tenn.: Broadman & Holman, 1993.

Craig, W. L. *Reasonable Faith: Christian Truth and Apologetics*. rev. ed. Wheaton, Ill.: Crossway, 1994.

Dembski, W. A. *Intelligent Design: The Bridge Between Science & Theology*. Downers Grove, Il.: InterVarsity, 1999.

_____., ed. *Mere Creation: Science, Faith & Intelligent Design*. Downers Grove, Ill.: InterVarsity, 1998.

Denton, M. *Evolution: A Theory in Crisis*. Bethesda, Md.: Adler & Adler, 1985.

Dyrness, W. A. *Christian Apologetics in a World Community*. Downers Grove, Ill.: InterVarsity, 1983.

Elwell, W. A., ed. *Baker Encyclopedia of the Bible*. Grand Rapids, Mich.: Baker, 1988.

Enroth, R. M. and Others. *A Guide to Cults & New Religions*. Downers Grove, Ill.: InterVarsity, 1983.

Erickson, M. J. *Christian Theology*. Grand Rapids, Mich.: Baker, 1987.

_____. *Postmodernizing the Faith: Evangelical Responses to the Challenge of Postmodernism*. Grand Rapids, Mich.: Baker, 1998.

Evans, C. S. *Pocket Dictionary of Apologetics & Philosophy: 300 Terms & Thinkers Clearly & Concisely Defined*. Downers Grove, Ill.: InterVarsity, 2002.

_____. *Baker Encyclopedia of Christian Apologetics*. Grand Rapids, Mich.: Baker, 1999.

_____. *Knowing the Truth About Creation: How It Happened and What It Means for Us*. General eds. J. I. Packer & Peter Kreeft. Ann Arbor, Mich.: Servant Books, 1989.

Geisler, N. L. *Miracles and the Modern Mind*. Grand Rapids, Mich.: Baker, 1992.

Geisler, N. L. & P. Bocchino, *Unshakeable Foundations: Contemporary Answers to Crucial Questions About the Christian Faith*. Minneapolis, Minn.: Bethany, 2001.

Geisler, N. L. & R. M. Brooks, *Come, Let Us Reason: An Introduction to Logical Thinking*. Grand Rapids, Mich.: Baker, 1998.

_____. *When Skeptics Ask: A Handbook on Christian Evidences*. Grand Rapids, Mich.: Baker, 1990.

Geisler, N. L. and Feinberg, P. D. *Introduction to Philosophy: A Christian Perspective*. Grand Rapids, Mich.: Baker, 2000.

Geivett, R. D. and G. R. Habermas, *In Defense of Miracles: A Comprehensive Case for God's Action in History*. Downers Grove, Ill.: InterVarsity, 1997.

Green, J. B., S. McKnight & I. H. Marshall, eds. *Dictionary of Jesus and the Gospels*. Downers Grove, Ill.: InterVarsity, 1992.

Groothuis, D. R. *Truth Decay: Defending Christianity Against the Challenges of Postmodernism*. Downers Grove, Ill.: InterVarsity, 2000.

_____. *Unmasking the New Age*. Downers Grove, Ill.: InterVarsity, 1986.

Grudem, W. *Systematic Theology: An Introduction to Biblical Doctrine*. Grand Rapids, Mich.: Zondervan, 1994.

Halverson, D. C., ed. *The Illustrated Guide to World Religions*. Bloomington, Minn.: Bethany, 1996.

Hanegraff, H. *Resurrection*. Nashville, Tenn.: Word, 2000.

_____. *The FACE That Demonstrates the Farce of Evolution*. Nashville, Tenn.: Word, 1998.

Heeren, F. *Show Me God: What the Message from Space Is Telling Us About God*. Wheeling, Ill.: Searchlight Publications, 1995.

House, H. W. *Charts of Cults, Sects, & Religious Movements*. Grand Rapids, Mich.: Zondervan, 2000.

Jeeves, M. A. and R. J. Berry, *Science, Life, and Christian Belief: A Survey of Contemporary Issues*. Grand Rapids, Mich.: Baker, 1998.

Johnson, P. E. *Darwin on Trial*. Downers Grove, Ill.: InterVarsity, 1993.

_____. *Defeating Darwinism by Opening Minds*. Downers Grove, Ill.: InterVarsity, 1997.

_____. *Objections Sustained: Subversive Essays on Evolution, Law & Culture*. Downers Grove, Ill.: InterVarsity, 1998.

_____. *Reason in the Balance: The Case Against NATURALISM in Science, Law & Education*. Downers Grove, Ill.: InterVarsity, 1995.

Larson, E. J. *Summer for the Gods: The Scopes Trial and the Continuing Evolution Debate*. New York: BasicBooks, 1997.

Lewis, C. S. *Miracles*. New York: Simon & Schuster, 1996.

Lewis, G. R. *Confronting the Cults*. Grand Rapids, Mich.: Baker, 1985.

Lewis, G. R. *Testing Christianity's Truth Claims*. Lanham, Md.: University Press, 1990.

Lewis, G. R. and B. A. Demarest, *Integrative Theology*. Grand Rapids, Mich.: Zondervan, 1996.

Marsden, G. M. *The Soul of the American University: From Protestant Establishment to Established Nonbelief.* New York: Oxford, 1994.

Martin, W. R. and R. Zacharias, rev. ed. *The Kingdom of the Cults.* Minneapolis: Bethany, 2003.

McDowell, J. *Handbook of Today's Religions.* San Bernardino: Here's Life Publishers, 1983.

_____. *More Than a Carpenter.* Wheaton, Ill.: Tyndale, 1977.

_____. *The New Evidence That Demands a Verdict.* Nashville, Tenn.: Thomas Nelson, 1999.

Monroe, K., ed. *Finding God at Harvard: Spiritual Journeys of Thinking Christians.* Grand Rapids, Mich.: Zondervan, 1996.

Moore, J. *The Darwin Legend.* Grand Rapids, Mich.: Baker, 1994.

Moreland, J. P. *Scaling the Secular City: A Defense of Christianity.* "Science and Christianity." Grand Rapids, Mich.: Baker, 1997.

_____., ed. *The Creation Hypothesis: Scientific Evidence for an Intelligent Designer.* Downers Grove, Ill.: InterVarsity, 1994.

_____. *Love Your God with All Your Mind: The Role of Reason in the Life of the Soul.* Colorado Springs, Colo.: NavPress, 1997.

Noll, M. A. *The Scandal of the Evangelical Mind.* Grand Rapids, Mich.: Eerdmans, 1994.

Osborne, G. R. *The Resurrection Narratives: A Redactional Study.* Grand Rapids, Mich.: Baker, 1984.

Ratzsch, D. *Science & Its Limits: The Natural Sciences in Christian Perspective.* Downers Grove, Ill.: InterVarsity, 2000.

Robertson, I. *What the Cults Believe.* Chicago: Moody, 1983.

Ross, H. *The Fingerprint of God.* Orange, Calif.: Promise Publishing, 1991.

Schaeffer, F. A. *A Christian Manifesto.* Westchester, Ill.: Crossway, 1982.

_____. *He Is There and He Is Not Silent.* Carol Stream, Ill.: Tyndale, 1972.

Sire, J. W. *The Universe Next Door: A Basic Worldview Catalog.* Downers Grove, Ill.: InterVarsity, 1976.

Strobel, L. *The Case for Christ: A Journalist's Personal Investigation of the Evidence for Christ.* Grand Rapids, Mich.: Zondervan, 1998.

_____. *The Case for Faith: A Journalist Investigates the Toughest Objections to Christianity.* Grand Rapids, Mich.: Zondervan, 2000.

Wegner, P. D. *The Journey from Texts to Translations: The Origin and Development of the Bible.* Grand Rapids, Mich.: Baker, 1999.

Wells, D. F. *Losing Our Virtue: Why the Church Must Recover Its Moral Vision.* Grand Rapids, Mich.: Eerdmans, 1998.

_____. *No Place for Truth: Or Whatever Happened to Evangelical Theology?* Grand Rapids, Mich.: Eerdmans, 1994.

Worthing, M. W. *God, Creation, and Contemporary Physics.* Augsburg Fortress, 1996.

Notes

1. A. W. Tozer, *The Knowledge of the Holy* (San Francisco: Harper San Francisco, 1961), p. 1.
2. Lee Strobel, *The Case for Christ* (Grand Rapids, Mich.: Zondervan, 1998), p. 60.
3. Geisler, N. L., *Baker Encyclopedia of Christian Apologetics* (Grand Rapids, Mich.: Baker, 1999), pp. 303-307.
4. For exact references, see N. L. Geisler, *Baker Encyclopedia of Apologetics* (Grand Rapids, Mich.: Baker, 1999), pp. 381-385. (Much of this chapter is based on that article.)
5. E. G. Louis Agassiz, Francis Bacon, Robert Boyle, George Cuvier, Michael Faraday, Johannes Kepler, Gregor Mendel, Samuel Morse, Isaac Newton, Blaise Pascal, Louis Pasteur, and William Ramsey to name a few.
6. Michael Denton, *Evolution: A Theory in Crisis* (Bethesda, Md.: Adler & Adler, 1985), p. 77.
7. A brief sample of individuals involved with the intelligent design movement accompanied by the location of their degrees is as follows: Michael Behe (Ph.D., biochemistry, University of Pennsylvania), David Berlinski (Ph.D., mathematics, Princeton University), Walter Bradley (Ph.D., mechanical engineering, University of Texas at Austin), William Lane Craig (Ph.D., philosophy, University

of Birmingham under John Hick; Ph.D., theology, University of Munich under Wolfhart Pannenberg), William Dembski (Ph.D., mathematics, University of Chicago; Ph.D., philosophy, University of Illinois at Chicago), Sigrid Hartwig-Scherer (Ph.D., physical anthropology, University of Zurich), Robert Kaita (Ph.D., physics, Rutgers University), Stephen Meyer (Ph.D., history and philosophy of science, Cambridge University), J. P. Moreland (Ph.D., philosophy, University of Southern California), Paul Nelson (Ph.D., philosophy, University of Chicago), Robert Newman (Ph.D., astrophysics, Cornell University), Del Ratzsch (Ph.D., philosophy, University of Massachusetts, Amherst), Henry F. Schaefer III (Ph.D., chemical physics, Stanford), Siegfried Scherer (Ph.D., biology, University of Konstanz), Jonathan Wells (Ph.D., religious studies, Yale; Ph.D., developmental biology, University of California at Berkeley). A sample of these individuals' credentials, publications, and awards truly is staggering.

8. Reputable astronomer and confessed agnostic Robert Jastrow, commenting on the scientific evidence for a beginning of the universe, remarks, "Three lines of evidence—the motions of the galaxies, the laws of thermodynamics, and the life story of the stars—pointed to one conclusion: all indicated that the Universe had a beginning." *God and the Astronomers* (New York: W. W. Norton, 1978), p. 111.

9. Most of the discussion in this essay is derived from chapter 3, "Information & the Origin of Life" by Walter L. Bradley and Charles B. Thaxton in J. P. Moreland, ed., *The Creation Hypothesis: Scientific Evidence for an Intelligent Designer* (Downers Grove, Ill.: InterVarsity, 1994), pp. 173-210.

10. Forty years later, Miller, then a professor of chemistry at the University of California at San Diego, said, "The problem of the origin of life has turned out to be much more difficult than I, and most other people, envisioned." J. Horgan, "In the Beginning . . . " *Scientific American*, February 1991, p. 117.

11. Hoyle quoted in *The Creation Hypothesis*, p. 191.

12. F. Crick, *Life Itself* (New York: Simon and Schuster, 1981).

13. The main points of this essay are taken from Kurt P. Wise, "The Origin of Life's Major Groups" in J. P. Moreland, ed., *The Creation Hypothesis: Scientific Evidence for an Intelligent Designer* (Downers Grove, Ill.: InterVarsity, 1994) and Siegfried Scherer, "Basic Types of Life" in William A. Dembski, ed., *Mere Creation: Science, Faith & Intelligent Design* (Downers Grove, Ill.: InterVarsity, 1998).

14. Much of this discussion is adapted from chapter 2 of Phillip E. Johnson's landmark critique of Darwinism, *Darwin on Trial* (Downers Grove, Ill.: InterVarsity, 1993), pp. 15-31.

15. Evolutionists distinguish between *macromutation* and that referred to as *micromutation*. Macromutations would be large-scale mutations, which evolutionists claim are impossible. Micromutations are small changes, which evolutionists argue, after accumulating over large periods of time, result in profound evolutionary change.

16. Darwin quoted in Johnson, pp. 36-37.

17. These conditions were taken from Johnson, p. 38.

18. Darwin quoted in Johnson, p. 46.

19. Johnson, p. 47.

20. Gould quoted in Normal L. Geisler, *The Baker Encyclopedia of Christian Apologetics* (Grand Rapids, Mich.: Baker, 1999), p. 226.

21. Eldredge quoted in Phillip E. Johnson, *Defeating Darwinism by Opening Minds* (Downers Grove, Ill.: InterVarsity, 1997), pp. 60-61.

22. Most people involved in human origins research would not purposefully deceive. But this example demonstrates the subjectivity of the trade and the lengths to which some will go to prove human evolution.

23. William R. Fix, *The Bone Peddlers: Selling Evolution* (New York: Macmillan, 1984), p. 12.

24. Johnson, p. 82.

25. Charles Darwin, *Origin of Species*, 6th ed. (New York: New York University Press, 1988), p. 154.

26. Michael J. Behe, *Darwin's Black Box: The Biochemical Challenge to Evolution* (New York: touchstone, 1996), p. 39.

27. This description is taken from Michael Behe's article, "Intelligent Design Theory as a Tool for Analyzing Biochemical Systems," in William A. Dembski, ed. p. 178.

28. For a detailed description of the irreducible complexity of the bacterial flagellum see Behe, pp. 180–81.

29. Behe, p. 187.

30. Behe, pp. 232-233.

31. Charles Darwin, *The Autobiography of Charles Darwin*, with original omissions restored. Edited by Nora Darwin Barlow (New York: W. W. Norton, 1993), p. 87.

32. Fred Heeren, *Show Me God: What the Message from Space Is Telling Us About God* (Wheeling, Ill.: Searchlight Publications, 1995), p. 179.

33. Stephen W. Hawking, *A Brief History of Time—From the Big Bang to Black Holes* (New York: Bantam Books, 1988), p. 125.

34. Heeren, p. 184.

35. Robert Jastrow, *God and the Astronomers* (New York: W. W. Norton, 1978), p. 15.

36. John W. Oller Jr. and John L. Omdahl, "Origin of the Human Language Capacity: In Whose Image?" in J. P. Moreland, ed., *The Creation Hypothesis,* p. 265.

37. This discussion and others in this section on miracles rely on chapter 5, "Questions About Miracles," in Norman L. Geisler and Ron Brooks, *When Skeptics Ask: A Handbook on Christian Evidences* (Grand Rapids, Mich.: Baker, 1990), pp. 86-95.

38. J. Ankenberg & J. Weldon, *Encyclopedia of Cults and New Religions* (Eugene, Ore.: Harvest House, 1999), p. 162.

39. Quoted in Ankenberg and Weldon, p. 175, from *The Watchtower,* July 4, 1973, p. 402.

40. Quoted in House, *Charts of Cults, Sects, & Religions Movements*, p. 163, from *Watchtower*, April 1, 1972, p. 197.

41. Quoted in Ankenberg & Weldon *Encyclopedia of Cults and New Religions,* p. 162.

42. Brigham Young, *Journal of Discourses* 7:333, quoted in House, p. 62.

43. Prophet Lorenzo Snow, as quoted in *The Gospel Through the Ages*, pp. 105-106, quoted in Martin, *The Kingdom of the Cults*, p. 236.

44. *Doctrine and Covenants*, 130:22, quoted in Martin, p. 236.

45 *Mormon Doctrine*, 1977 ed., p. 516, quoted in House, p. 63.

46. Apostle James Talmage in *The Articles of Faith*, ed., 1974, p. 473, quoted in Martin, p. 245.

47. Apostle Orson Hyde, *Journal of Discourses,* 2:210, quoted in House, p. 66.

48. Jess L. Christensen, *A Sure Foundation*, p. 224, quoted in Ankenberg and Weldon, p. 299.
49. Martin, pp. 151-153.
50. *Science and Health*, p. 107, quoted in McDowell and Stewart, *Handbook of Today's Religions*, p. 124.
51. Martin, pp. 377-378; Ankenberg, p. 455.
52. Martin, pp. 353-355.
53. Martin, pp. 351, 360.
54. Enroth, *A Guide to Cults & New Religions*, p. 177.
55. House, p. 105.
56. House, p. 122.
57. www.watchman.org/profile/fampro.htm (accessed October 28, 2004).

Author

Dr. Rick Cornish previously taught theology for seven years in the former Soviet Union. A graduate of Denver Seminary, Rick lives in Minnesota with his wife, Tracy. They have two sons, Scott and Ben—the original and most important audience for this book—who are both in college.